CAMBRIDGE

Environmental Management

for Cambridge IGCSE™ and O Level

WORKBOOK

Gary Skinner, Ken Crafer, Melissa Turner,
Ann Skinner & John Stacey

Second edition

CAMBRIDGE
UNIVERSITY PRESS & ASSESSMENT

Shaftesbury Road, Cambridge CB2 8EA, United Kingdom

One Liberty Plaza, 20th Floor, New York, NY 10006, USA

477 Williamstown Road, Port Melbourne, VIC 3207, Australia

314–321, 3rd Floor, Plot 3, Splendor Forum, Jasola District Centre, New Delhi – 110025, India

103 Penang Road, #05–06/07, Visioncrest Commercial, Singapore 238467

Cambridge University Press & Assessment is a department of the University of Cambridge.

We share the University's mission to contribute to society through the pursuit of education, learning and research at the highest international levels of excellence.

www.cambridge.org
Information on this title: www.cambridge.org/9781009808965

© Cambridge University Press & Assessment 2025

First published 2017
Second edition 2025
20 19 18 17 16 15 14 13 12 11 10 9 8 7 6 5 4 3 2 1

Printed in Malaysia by Vivar Printing

A catalogue record for this publication is available from the British Library

ISBN 978-1-009-80900-9 Student's Book with Digital Access (2 years)
ISBN 978-1-009-80902-3 Digital Student's Book (2 years)
ISBN 978-1-009-80903-0 Student's Book eBook
ISBN 978-1-009-80896-5 Workbook with Digital Access (2 years)
ISBN 978-1-009-80899-6 Digital Teacher's Resource (2 years)
ISBN 978-1-009-80898-9 Teacher's Resource Access Card

Additional resources for this publication at www.cambridge.org/9781009808965

For EU product safety concerns, contact us at Calle de José Abascal, 56, 1°, 28003 Madrid, Spain, or email eugpsr@cambridge.org.

2024 Cambridge Dedicated Teacher Awards

Our **Cambridge Dedicated Teacher Awards** are an opportunity to show appreciation for the incredible work teachers do every day.

Thank you to everyone who nominated this year; we have been inspired and moved by all of your stories. Well done to all of our nominees for your dedication to learning and for inspiring the next generation of thinkers, leaders and innovators.

Congratulations to our winners!

Global Winner
South East Asia & Pacific
Sydney Engelbert
Keningau Vocational College, Malaysia

East Asia
Pengfei Jiang
Zhuji Ronghuai Foreign Language School, China

Pakistan
Saeeda Salim
SISA - School of International Studies in Sciences & Arts, Pakistan

South Asia
Meena Mishra
Dr Sarvepalli Radhakrishnan International School, India

Middle East and North Africa
Gina Justus
Our Own English High school- Sharjah- Girls, United Arab Emirates

Sub-Saharan Africa
Tajudeen Odufeso
Isara Secondary School, Isara Remo, Nigeria

Europe
Aynur Bayazit
Menekşe Ahmet Yalçınkaya Kindergarten, Türkiye

Latin America & the Caribbean
Ramon Majé Floriano
Montessori sede San Francisco, Colombia

North America
Marisa Santos
Seminole Ridge Community High School, United States

For more information about our dedicated teachers and their stories, go to
dedicatedteacher.cambridge.org

CAMBRIDGE

Endorsement statement

Endorsement indicates that a resource has passed Cambridge International Education's rigorous quality-assurance process and is suitable to support the delivery of their syllabus. However, endorsed resources are not the only suitable materials available to support teaching and learning, and are not essential to achieve the qualification. For the full list of endorsed resources to support this syllabus, visit www.cambridgeinternational.org/endorsedresources

Any example answers to questions taken from past question papers, practice questions, accompanying marks and mark schemes included in this resource have been written by the authors and are for guidance only. They do not replicate examination papers. In examinations the way marks are awarded may be different. Any references to assessment and/ or assessment preparation are the publisher's interpretation of the syllabus requirements. Examiners will not use endorsed resources as a source of material for any assessment set by Cambridge International Education.

While the publishers have made every attempt to ensure that advice on the qualification and its assessment is accurate, the official syllabus, specimen assessment materials and any associated assessment guidance materials produced by the awarding body are the only authoritative source of information and should always be referred to for definitive guidance.

Our approach is to provide teachers with access to a wide range of high-quality resources that suit different styles and types of teaching and learning.

For more information about the endorsement process, please visit www.cambridgeinternational.org/endorsed-resources

> Contents

> How to use this series

We offer a comprehensive, flexible array of resources for the Cambridge IGCSE™ and O Level Environmental Management syllabuses. We provide targeted support and practice for the specific challenges we've heard that learners face: learning a new subject with English as a second language; application of science and data skills; contextualising learning; and more.

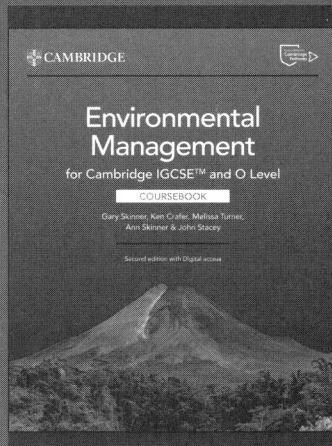

This Coursebook provides coverage of the full Cambridge IGCSE™ and O Level Environmental Management syllabuses. Each chapter explains facts and concepts, and uses relevant real-world examples of environmental management principles to bring the subject to life. Together with a focus on active learning opportunities and assessment of learning, the Coursebook prepares learners for all aspects of their study. At the end of each chapter, examination-style practice questions offer opportunities for learners to apply their learning. Answers can be found on Cambridge GO via the activation code found on the inside of the front cover.

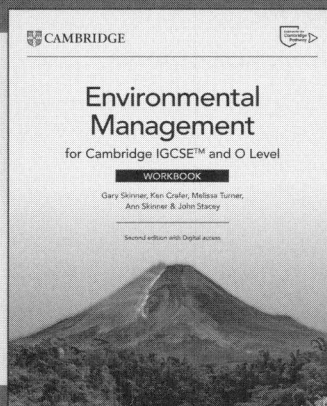

The skills-focused Workbook has been carefully constructed to help learners develop the skills that they need as they progress through their Cambridge IGCSE™ and O Level Environmental Management courses, providing further practice of key topics in the Coursebook. The Workbook enables independent learning and is ideal for use in class or as homework. Answers can be found on Cambridge GO via the activation code found on the inside of the front cover.

Our Digital Teacher's Resource contains detailed guidance for all topics of the syllabus, including common misconceptions and identifying areas where learners might need extra support, as well as an engaging bank of lesson ideas for each syllabus topic. Tests, worksheets and additional case studies with questions are provided, ready to hand out in your lessons. Differentiation is emphasised with advice for identification of different learner needs and suggestions of appropriate interventions to support and stretch learners. Answers for all components are accessible to teachers on the Cambridge GO platform.

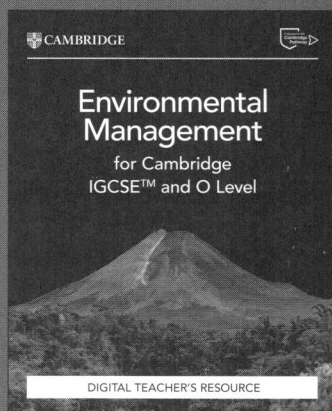

> How to use this book

Throughout this book, you will notice lots of different features that will help your learning. These are explained below. Answers are accessible to teachers and learners for free by activating your digital code on the inside cover of this book on the Cambridge GO website.

Exercises

These question-based exercises help you to test your knowledge and practise skills that are important for your success in Cambridge IGCSE and O Level Environmental Management. There are exercises for all key topics and subtopics.

KEY WORDS

Key vocabulary for the syllabus is highlighted in the text when it is first introduced. Definitions are given in the margin and can also be found in the Glossary at the back of the book.

LEARNING INTENTIONS

Learning intentions indicate the key skills you will be focusing on in each exercise.

TIPS

These are helpful reminders or notes that will give advice on skills or methodology. You will find them most often near activities or questions, where they will be directly relevant to the task. Different tip types include: Science, Maths, Sustainability, Practical, Problem solving and Critical thinking.

SELF-ASSESSMENT

At the end of some exercises, you will find opportunities to help you assess your own work, or that of your classmates, and consider how you can improve the way you learn.

> Skills grid

The information in this section is based on the Cambridge International Education syllabus. You should always refer to the appropriate syllabus document for the year of examination to confirm the details and for more information. The syllabus document is available on the website: www.cambridgeinternational.org.

This grid maps the workbook exercises to the Cambridge IGCSE and O Level Environmental Management assessment objectives.

Assessment objective	Workbook chapters							
	1	2	3	4	5	6	7	8
AO1 Knowledge with understanding								
Phenomena, facts, definitions, concepts and theories		2.1, 2.2, 2.3, 2.4, 2.5, 2.6, 2.7	3.1, 3.2, 3.3	4.1, 4.2, 4.3, 4.4, 4.5, 4.6, 4.7	5.1, 5.2, 5.3, 5.4	6.1, 6.2, 6.3, 6.4, 6.5	7.1, 7.2, 7.3, 7.4, 7.5	8.2, 8.4, 8.5
Vocabulary, terminology and conventions	1.2	2.1, 2.2, 2.4, 2.5	3.1, 3.2	4.1, 4.2, 4.3, 4.6, 4.7, 4.8	5.2, 5.4	6.1, 6.4	7.1, 7.4	8.1, 8.2, 8.3
Strategies for managing the environment locally, regionally and globally		2.2, 2.3, 2.4, 2.5, 2.6	3.2, 3.3	4.1, 4.2, 4.4, 4.6, 4.7, 4.8	5.2, 5.3, 5.4	6.3, 6.4	7.2, 7.3, 7.4, 7.5	8.5
AO2 Handling information and problem-solving								
Locate, select, organise and present information from a variety of sources	1.3, 1.4	2.7		4.3, 4.7	5.2, 5.3	6.2, 6.3, 6.4, 6.5	7.4, 7.5	8.3, 8.4
Translate information and evidence from one form to another	1.2, 1.3, 1.4	2.5, 2.7	3.2	4.2	5.2, 5.3	6.2, 6.4, 6.5	7.2, 7.5	8.2, 8.3, 8.5
Manipulate numerical and other data	1.3	2.3, 2.4, 2.6	3.2	4.2, 4.5	5.2	6.2, 6.3, 6.4, 6.5	7.2, 7.5	8.1, 8.3, 8.4
Interpret data, identify patterns and describe relationships	1.3, 1.4	2.4, 2.5	3.1, 3.2, 3.3	4.6, 4.7	5.2, 5.3, 5.4	6.3, 6.4	7.2, 7.3, 7.5	8.1, 8.2, 8.3, 8.4
Solve problems, including some of a quantitative nature	1.3, 1.4	2.3	3.1	4.6	5.2, 5.4	6.4, 6.5	7.5	

Assessment objective	Workbook chapters							
	1	2	3	4	5	6	7	8
AO3 Investigation skills and making judgements								
Plan fieldwork investigations and how to do them safely	1.1, 1.2	2.3, 2.6	3.1	4.3, 4.6	5.3	6.5		
Evaluate methods, identify limitations and suggest improvements to fieldwork investigations	1.1, 1.2	2.3	3.1	4.6	5.3			
Suggest reasoned explanations for phenomena, patterns and relationships	1.4	2.4	3.1	4.3, 4.6, 4.7	5.2	6.2, 6.3		8.1, 8.2
Make reasoned judgements and form conclusions based on evidence	1.4	2.3	3.2	4.3, 4.6	5.3	6.4, 6.5	7.5	8.4

> Introduction

This Cambridge IGCSE™ and O Level Environmental Management Workbook has been written to help you develop the skills you need for your course for Cambridge IGCSE and O Level Environmental Management (0680/5014). To succeed in this course, you need to have an excellent factual knowledge of all the topics in the syllabus and you also need to be able to handle data. As you work through the book, chapter by chapter, you will develop the relevant skills needed and gain the confidence to use them yourself. The exercises in this Workbook provide opportunities to practise the following skills:

- finding information in text, diagrams or graphs, and then using the information to answer questions

- changing information from one form to another – for example, using words to describe a graph, or creating a pie chart to represent data

- using technical vocabulary correctly

- doing calculations

- using information to identify patterns and trends

- suggesting explanations for unfamiliar data or other information provided, using the knowledge you have gained in your course

- making predictions or hypotheses.

The exercises in each chapter will help you develop these skills by applying them to new contexts. The chapters are arranged in the same order as the chapters in the Cambridge IGCSE and O Level Environmental Management Coursebook. Like the Coursebook, there is a dedicated skills chapter that will help you to practice the skills you have learned, before applying them to each individual topic. Each exercise in the Workbook has an introduction that outlines the skills you will be developing.

We hope that this Workbook will help you succeed in your course, give you the necessary skills to help you with your future studies and inspire you to have a love of the environment and its management.

Note on maps: *The boundaries and names shown, the designations used and the presentation of material on any maps contained in this resource do not imply official endorsement or acceptance by Cambridge University Press concerning the legal status of any country, territory, or area or any of its authorities, or of the delimitation of its frontiers or boundaries.*

> Chapter 1

Key skills in Environmental Management

> Planning an investigation

Exercise 1.1

LEARNING INTENTIONS
In this exercise you will:
• identify some key fieldwork apparatus
• plan an investigation from a given **aim**
• show your understanding of **sampling techniques** and strategies.

KEY WORDS

aim: the purpose of an investigation

sampling technique: the method of collecting data in an investigation

hypothesis: a statement on a topic being investigated

dependent variable: the variable that is measured in an experiment

sampling strategy: the way in which data is collected, either randomly or systematically

1   Identify each piece of apparatus.

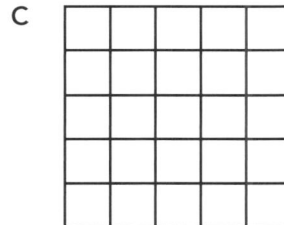

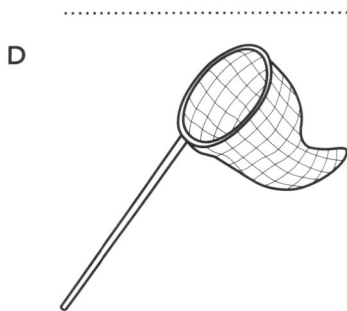

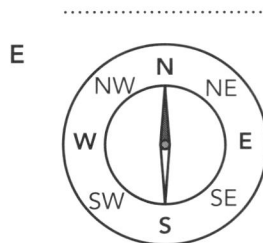

A

B

C

....

....

....

D

E

F

....

....

....

2　**a**　An investigation has the aim 'to investigate the effects of soil pH on the height of plants near to a mine waste tip'. Suggest a suitable **hypothesis** for this investigation.

....

....

b　Identify the **dependent variable** in this investigation.

....

c　The scientist carrying out this investigation decided to use a 60-metre transect. What is a transect?

....

....

d　Name one other piece of apparatus the scientist could use in this investigation.

....

e　Suggest a suitable **sampling strategy** for this investigation.

....

f　Describe how the scientist could use the transect to investigate the effects of soil pH on the height of plants near the mine waste tip.

....

....

....

....

3　A scientist wanted to survey a field for insect pests.

a　What sampling technique would the scientist use?

....

b　Explain how each of the following sampling strategies could be applied to this investigation.

Random: ....

....

Systematic: ....

....

c Describe how the scientist collects the data. Include the apparatus the scientist would use.

....

....

....

....

d Suggest what the limitations of using this apparatus might be.

....

....

....

....

> Collecting and recording data

Exercise 1.2

LEARNING INTENTIONS

In this exercise you will:

- identify types of data
- consider accuracy in an investigation
- identify and analyse the variables in an investigation
- identify health and safety concerns
- suggest improvements to a **questionnaire**
- record information in a tally chart and a table.

KEY WORDS

questionnaire: a written list of questions that people are asked so that information can be collected

independent variable: the variable that is deliberately changed in an experiment

1   Cadmium, a heavy-metal pollutant from industrial activity, was found to be contaminating streams, rivers and lakes in an area. In an investigation into the effect of this on fish growth, the hypothesis tested was: 'The growth rate of fish will be lower in the presence of higher heavy-metal concentrations in the water.'

What type of data will be obtained when testing this hypothesis?
Circle the correct answer.

qualitative   quantitative

2   To test the hypothesis, the mass of the fish would need to be calculated over a period of time. Mass is calculated by weighing the fish on an accurate balance (Figure 1.1).

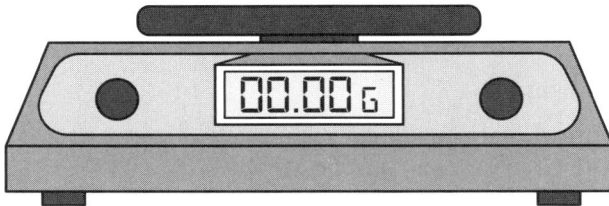

Figure 1.1: A balance used for weighing.

a   What is meant by 'accuracy'?

....

....

b   How can you ensure accuracy when using a balance?

....

....

KEY WORD
control variable: in an experiment, a factor that is kept constant

3 A student was asked to find out if the cadmium was also contaminating irrigation water and affecting crop growth.

The student chose a large field where no natural heavy-metal pollution was affecting the irrigation water. Four concentrations of cadmium were investigated. The field was divided into four plots, and a rice crop was grown in each plot (Figure 1.2). Each plot was irrigated with pure water or water contaminated with the cadmium. The total mass of rice harvested was measured.

Figure 1.2: A rice field divided into plots.

a Suggest a hypothesis for this investigation.

....

....

b Identify the independent and dependent variables.

Independent variable: ....

Dependent variable: ....

c Name **two control variables** in this investigation that are to do with the rice crop.

....

....

d Name **two** control variables in this investigation to do with the physical (abiotic) environment in which the rice is growing.

....

....

e Explain how the design of the investigation will ensure, as far as possible, that the variables you have named in part d will be the same in all four plots.

....

....

....

4 Suggest **three** potential health and safety issues the student should be aware of when collecting this data, and how these issues can be managed.

....

....

....

....

....

....

5 In a follow-up investigation, people in the area were asked about their concerns, using a questionnaire. Here are some of the questions they were asked:

A How concerned are you about the pollution of your water supply with heavy metals?

very concerned   **concerned**   **don't know**

not concerned

B Please tell me about any incidents in which you think you were affected by using water polluted with heavy metal.

C How much water do you drink in a day?

<1 litre   **about 1 litre**   **>1 litre**

D Who do you blame for the heavy-metal pollution?

a Which questions (A to D) are open questions and which are closed questions?

Open questions: ....

Closed questions: ....

b Suggest a better order for the questions in the questionnaire. Explain your answer.

....

....

c Suggest **two** further questions to be added to the questionnaire – one closed question and one open question.

Closed question: ....

....

Open question: ....

....

d State reasons why a pilot survey should be conducted.

....

....

....

6 a A student wanted to investigate the effects of cadmium pollution on female fish reproduction and growth. The student counted 73 eggs in a one square metre area and used a tally chart to count the fish eggs. Write down the tally chart record of this number of eggs.

b In the same investigation seven concentrations of cadmium (ppm), including zero were used. The number of eggs at each concentration were counted. Draw a table in which the results of this experiment could be recorded.

> Presenting data

Exercise 1.3

KEY WORDS

line graph: a graph showing the relationship between two quantitative variables

bar chart: a graph showing the relationship between a categoric variable and a quantitative variable

trend: a general pattern in data showing an increase, decrease or remaining constant, when smaller changes are ignored

1 a A scientist wanted to investigate how the mass of fish caught in tonnes each year were affected by the presence of cadmium concentrations in the water. The results are shown in Table 1.1.

Year	Mass of fish caught / tonnes
2014	65
2015	60
2016	57
2017	55
2018	50
2019	46
2020	41
2021	34
2022	30
2023	27

Table 1.1: Mass of fish caught in tonnes, 2014–2023.

Draw a line graph to show the data.

b Describe the **trend** on the graph.

....

....

....

c Calculate the percentage decrease in the fish catch between 2014 and 2023. Write your answer to one decimal place.

....

2   Another investigation measured the percentage of various species of fish in which egg laying was reduced by the cadmium pollution. The results are shown in Table 1.2.

Effect of cadmium on fish egg laying	Percentage of fish species affected
Unaffected	7
Slightly affected	23
Significantly affected	52
Very badly affected	18

Table 1.2: Percentage of fish in which egg laying was reduced by cadmium pollution.

a   State which data presentation technique you would use to display this data. Explain your answer. Give an alternative method that would also be suitable.

....

....

....

....

....

....

b   The data on which this categorisation was based are shown in Table 1.3.

Number of eggs laid as a percentage of the number laid with no cadmium	Number of species laying this percentage of normal number of eggs
100–80	2
<80–60	15
<60–40	17
<40–20	29
<20–0	59

Table 1.3: Categorisation data for the study of egg laying in fish in waters polluted by cadmium.

Calculate how many species of fish were investigated.

c   Which method of data presentation would you use with the data in part b?
     Explain your answer.

     ....

     ....

3   The bar chart in Figure 1.3 shows the state of global fish stocks in 2024.
     Complete the bar chart to show 17% of global fish stocks have been
     moderately exploited.

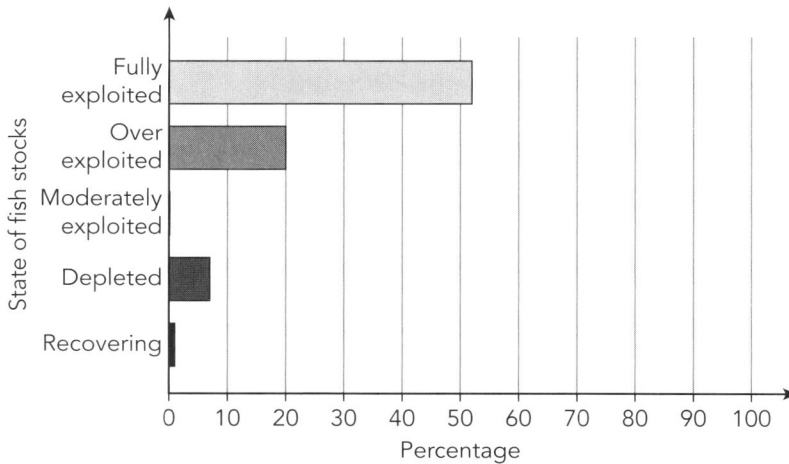

Figure 1.3: The state of global fish stocks, 2024.

> Analysing data

Exercise 1.4

LEARNING INTENTIONS

In this exercise you will:

- work out percentages

- create a **scatter graph** from given data

- identify trends and pattern of **correlation**

- calculate **mean** and **range**.

KEY WORDS

scatter graph:
a graph with points representing amounts or numbers on it, often with a line joining the points

correlation:
a pattern between two variables

1 Globally, it has been estimated that 200 million tonnes of fish and seafood were produced in 2024. China produced 62.24 million tonnes of fish and seafood. What percentage does China produce? Write your answer to one decimal place.

....

2 A student wanted to see if a relationship existed between fish mass (kg) and length (cm).

a Draw a scatter graph to show this relationship, using the data in Table 1.4.

Fish mass / kg	Length / cm
2	50
2	55
3	60
4	65
5	70
6	75
7	80
9	85
10	90
12	95

Table 1.4: The relationship between fish mass and length.

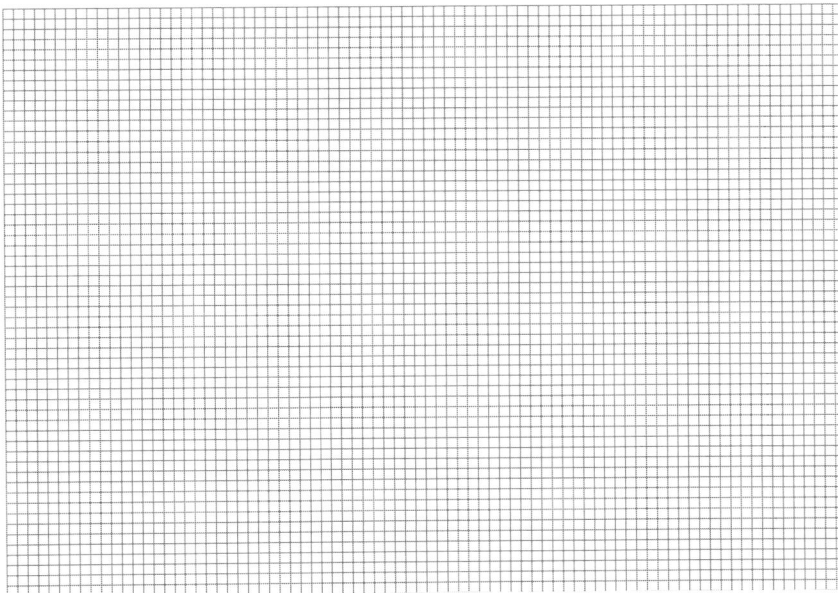

b Describe the trend shown.

....

....

c Describe the correlation shown.

....

d Is this graph **directly proportional** or **inversely proportional**?

....

e Give **one** advantage of using a scatter graph to present data.

....

....

PEER ASSESSMENT

Share your graphs in small groups. Check each graph for the following:

- Are the x- and y-axes labelled correctly?

- Is the linear scale sensible with plotted points that cover at least half of the grid?

- Are all the plots correct?

3 Five female fish were investigated at each of seven heavy-metal concentrations. The following results were found at a heavy-metal concentration of 2.

- Female 1: 79 eggs

- Female 2: 98 eggs

- Female 3: 64 eggs

- Female 4: 90 eggs

- Female 5: 79 eggs

Calculate the mean and the range of this data.

Mean: ....

Range: ....

Chapter 2

Natural resources

> The formation and characteristics of rocks

Exercise 2.1

LEARNING INTENTIONS

In this exercise you will:

- identify stages in the **rock cycle**
- Define key terms in the rock cycle
- classify rocks according to their permeability
- describe how sedimentary rock is formed.

1 Insert these words into the correct spaces on Figure 2.1.

igneous rocks   **sedimentary rocks**   **weathering**

metamorphic rocks   **transportation**   **magma**

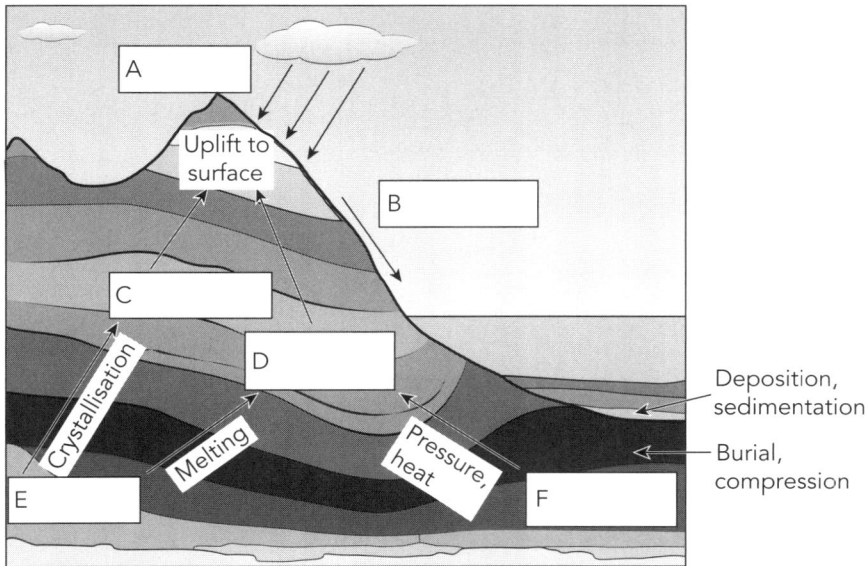

Figure 2.1: Part of the rock cycle.

KEY WORDS

rock cycle: a representation of the changes between the three rock types and the processes causing them

igneous rock: rock made during volcanic processes

sedimentary rock: a rock formed from material derived from the weathering of other rocks or the accumulation of dead plants and animals

weathering: the processes that cause rock to be broken down into smaller particles

transportation: the process by which rock particles are moved to another location

2 Draw lines to link the following 'M' words with their correct definitions.

magma	Naturally occurring inorganic substances with a specific chemical composition.
mineral	Molten rock below the surface of Earth.
metamorphic	An example of a metamorphic rock.
marble	Rocks formed from existing rocks by a combination of heat and pressure.

3 Classify each rock by its type by writing it in the correct column of the table.

basalt   limestone   sandstone   marble   slate   granite   shale

Igneous	Metamorphic	Sedimentary

4 a Complete the sentence.

'Permeability' means ....

....

b Which of the rocks in the table are permeable and which are impermeable?

Permeable: ....

....

Impermeable: ....

....

5 Describe how a sedimentary rock forms.

....

....

....

....

....

....

> Extraction methods

Exercise 2.2

1   Insert the three words below into the gaps in the following sentence so that it makes an accurate statement.

rock   ore   minerals

The .... is found in .... and is made up of one or

more .... or metals.

2   A new source of minerals has been found. It is decided that the minerals should be extracted from this new source. Explain how the following three factors might affect the way the minerals might be extracted.

    a   Geology: ....

       ....

       ....

       ....

    b   Environmental impact: ....

       ....

       ....

       ....

    c   Market price for the minerals: ....

       ....

       ....

       ....

3 Complete the table to identify details about three different ways of extracting rocks, ores and minerals.

Extraction type	Example	Advantages	Disadvantages
Surface extraction			
Subsurface extraction			
Biological extraction			

› The impacts of extraction

Exercise 2.3

LEARNING INTENTIONS

In this exercise you will:

- explore the effects of quarrying on the local area
- suggest extraction methods that will cause the least environmental damage
- consider ways of disposing of mining waste safely
- investigate tree planting as a strategy for managing landscapes damaged by extraction.

KEY WORD

ecosystem: all the living things (biotic components) together with all the non-living things (abiotic components) in an area

1   Figure 2.2 shows part of a mine used for the extraction of stone known as
    a quarry. The quarry produces large blocks of stone that will be carved for
    important buildings.

Figure 2.2: A stone quarry for Portland stone.

a   How might the extraction of this stone benefit local people?

    ....

    ....

    ....

    ....

    ....

    ....

b   Describe **three** negative impacts the development of this quarry could have on
    the local community.

    ....

    ....

    ....

    ....

    ....

    ....

c Suggest **three** ways in which the local **ecosystem** might be affected by the development of the quarry.

....

....

....

....

....

....

2 The removal of topsoil has resulted in the local extinction of a small flowering plant. Suggest why this loss may be important.

....

....

....

....

3 State which of the three extraction methods listed in Exercise 2.2 question 3 is likely to be the most effective for the mining of stone but also have the least impact on a rare plant. Give a reason for your answer.

Extraction method: ....

Reason: ....

....

....

4   It is a mining company's responsibility to ensure that a mining site is left in good condition once excavation has been completed. A plan for this restoration often has to be submitted before a licence will be granted for extraction to take place.

Evaluate the suitability of the following proposals for an old site with a large bowl-like crater (Figure 2.3). Include the strengths and weakness of each proposal.

Figure 2.3: An area of land that has been damaged by the extraction of natural resources.

Potential use	Evaluation
Waste disposal site for household waste	
Planting trees and sowing wild flower seeds in the area	
Conversion of the crater into a racetrack	
Flood the crater for use as a fish farm	
Develop a shopping centre in the crater	

5   a   Rock, ore and mineral extraction also creates a large volume of waste. State **one** method of disposing of mining waste safely.

....

b Describe the checks a mining company should do to ensure that the waste materials are not causing damage to the local environment.

....

....

....

....

....

....

6 Mining companies will often plant trees to help restore a site. It is observed that the growth of these trees is very slow compared to trees planted at other sites. Suggest **three** reasons for this.

a ....

....

b ....

....

c ....

....

7 Tree planting can be labour intensive. In Canada, a company pays US$0.11 for each young tree planted as part of its reforestation programme.

a Calculate how much a worker would earn if they planted 1600 trees per day.

US$..............................

b A survey of the site identified that only 40% of these young trees survive for more than five years. Calculate the number of trees planted by the worker per day that have survived more than five years.

Number of trees: ....

TIP

Remember to always show your working. Depending on the question, you may still get credit for the method even if you make an error in the calculation itself.

8   A manager plans to look at the survival rate of trees to see whether the percentage could be increased. Outline an investigation that could be done to evaluate whether additional training given to tree planters would have an effect. Make sure you put the steps of the investigation in a logical order.

....

....

....

....

....

....

....

....

....

....

TIP

Some tasks may present you with a scenario that you have not faced before. Remember, you can apply your knowledge of other investigations to the new situation.

› Sustainable management of rocks, ores and minerals

Exercise 2.4

LEARNING INTENTIONS

In this exercise you will:

* revise some key terminology relating to rocks, ores and minerals

* explain some issues related to metal recycling

* present and analyse data related to types of waste products.

KEY WORD

fossil fuel: a carbon-based fuel, formed over many millions of years from the decay of living matter

1 Use the clues to complete the 'across' words in the puzzle. When you have finished, the first initial of each answer will reveal a method for ensuring that mineral resources are used appropriately. Some of the letters in each word have been put in to help you.

1		E							
2					C				
3		O							
4			E						
5			U						
6		E					T		
7		F					N		

1 An efficient way of preventing the need to manufacture an item again. (5)

2 Removing the useful metal from ore. (7)

3 A widely mined **fossil fuel**. (4)

4 The percentage of a mineral obtained from the rock. (5)

5 The method of breaking down large rocks into smaller pieces to obtain the minerals. (5)

6 A way that a government can control the use and extraction of minerals. (11)

7 The effective use of extracted minerals. (9)

Method: ....

2 Suggest **four** reasons why the mass of recycled metals used in industry may be less than the amount potentially available.

a ....
....

b ....
....

c ....
....

d ....
....

3 State **three** ways that governments could ensure that people recycle a higher proportion of metals in the home.

a ....

....

b ....

....

c ....

....

4 Table 2.1 shows the result of a study of the types of waste produced by a city in Argentina.

Waste type	Proportion of total waste (%)
Organic (food and plant)	42
Glass	6
Metals	4
Paper and card	27
Rocks and concrete	12
Other	9

Table 2.1: Types of waste produced in a city in Argentina.

a Use the information in Table 2.1 to complete the pie chart.

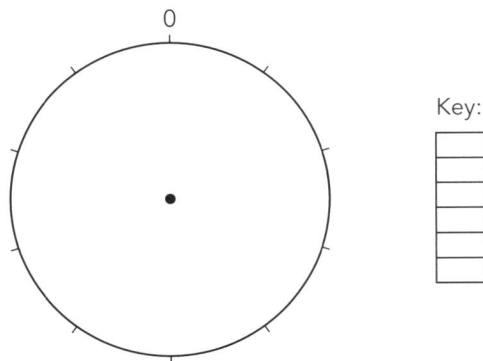

0

Key:

TIP

Make sure your pie chart follows these rules:

Sectors in rank order.

Largest sector beginning at noon and proceeding clockwise.

Data categorised as 'other' should also be plotted in rank order.

b What type of waste is used least in this city?

....

c   Looking at this data, a student concludes that there is little benefit
in recycling a material that is less than 10% of the total waste.
Suggest reasons why the recycling of materials that are less
than 10% of the total waste is still beneficial.

....

....

....

....

....

....

....

....

SELF-ASSESSMENT

How confident do you feel about drawing a pie chart?
Tick the column that best describes how well you completed each feature.

Feature	I forgot to add this feature	I added this feature but could do this better	I completed this feature well
I started my plotting at the top of the pie (12 o'clock).			
I plotted the segments in a clockwise direction.			
I plotted the segments from largest to smallest, with the 'others' section last.			
I plotted the segments accurately using a ruler for straight lines.			
I completed the key.			
The shading on the key and the pie chart match and are different to all the other segments.			

› Sources of energy
Exercise 2.5

LEARNING INTENTIONS

In this exercise you will:

- complete a puzzle using key terminology relating to energy resources

- describe how fossil fuels are formed

- classify different energy sources

- explain the limitations of fossil fuels

- describe how **wind power** and **wave power** generate electricity

- suggest reasons why people may not be in favour of a **hydro-electric** scheme

- show your understanding of how different factors affect energy demand

- analyse data related to energy use.

KEY WORDS

wind power: electricity generation using a wind turbine

wave power: the use of changes in the height of a body of water to generate electricity

hydro-electric: the generation of electricity using flowing water

solar power: harnessing energy from sunlight

natural gas: a naturally occurring flammable gas that contains carbon; the most common example of natural gas is methane

turbine: a machine, often containing fins, that is made to revolve by the use of gas, steam or air

petroleum: a liquid mixture of carbon-containing chemicals that is present in some rocks, which is extracted and refined to produce fuels such as petrol and diesel oil

1   Solve the clues to complete the word puzzle about resources and energy generation.

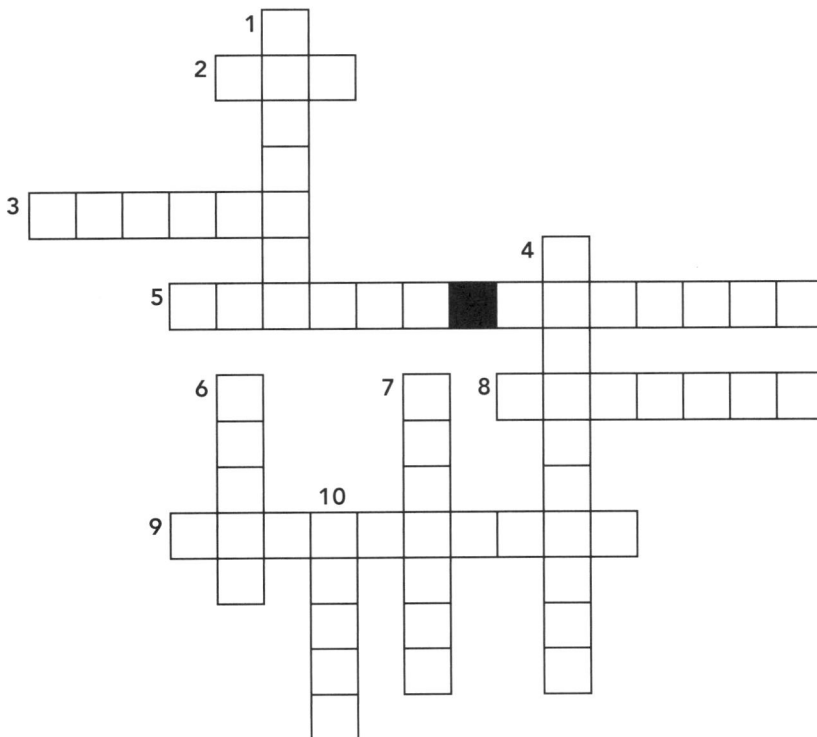

Across

2   Source of **solar power**. (3)

3   A way of describing an energy source that is limited in amount. (6)

5   Gas produced from the combustion of coal. (6, 7)

8   Main component of **natural gas**. (7)

9   Energy resource that uses underground heat. (10)

Down

1   A finite energy resource that does not produce carbon dioxide. (7)

4   Biofuel fermented from plants. (10)

6   This is heated to produce steam to drive a **turbine**. (5)

7   The energy an object has because of its motion. (7)

10   Renewable energy source that uses a change in water level. (5)

2   Use words from the list to complete the passage about fossil fuels and their formation. The words may be used once, more than once or not at all.

organic   plants   rock   pressure   sediment   ground

radiation   coal

Fossil fuels are not actually made from fossils, but it is a useful term to describe

the amount of time it takes to produce them. Fossils fuels are produced

from the decay of .... and animals. These remains formed

.... matter that became covered in layers of sediment.

Over millions of years, and buried deep in the .... by the

addition of further layers of sediment, the organic material is subjected to high

.... and heat. The precise conditions, and the type of animal and

plant material available, will determine whether ...., **petroleum**

(oil) or natural gas is produced.

3 Write the following energy sources in the correct column of the table.

petroleum   geothermal   hydro-electric   wave   coal   nuclear

tidal   natural gas   wind   solar   biofuels

Non-renewable energy sources	Renewable energy sources

SELF-ASSESSMENT

Being able to classify energy resources accurately is an important skill.
How confident do you feel about this?
Tick the column to assess your confidence in each skill.

Skill	Very confident	Fairly confident	I need more practice
I can name **two** energy resources that need to be combusted.			
I can name **three** energy resources that are dependent on weather conditions.			
I can name **four** non-renewable energy resources.			
I can name **five** renewable energy resources.			
I can name **six** energy resources that do not emit greenhouse gases when used.			

Compare your scores with a partner. Challenge your partner to name the examples they have used against one of the skills, then allow them to challenge you on another skill to check if you are both right.

4   Explain why it is not possible to produce more coal or petroleum simply by collecting organic waste matter, which is easily available.

....

....

....

....

5   Describe how a wind turbine (Figure 2.4) is used to produce electricity.

....

....

....

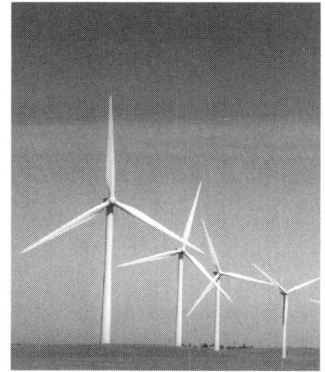

Figure 2.4: A wind turbine.

6   Figure 2.5 shows how electricity can be generated from wave power.

Key:

↑   Direction of wave/water

§   Direction of air flow

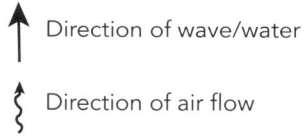

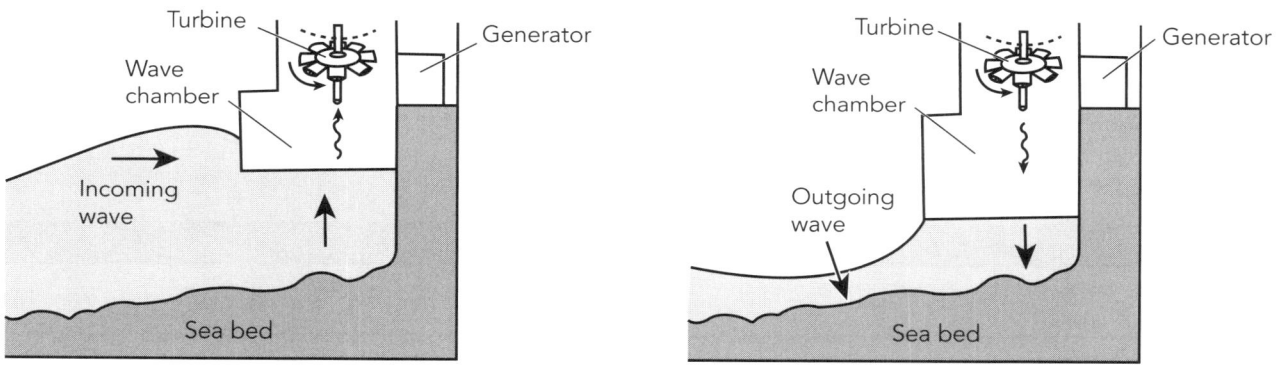

Figure 2.5: A wave turbine in action.

Use the diagram to describe how wave power is used to generate electricity.

....

....

....

....

....

....

....

....

TIP

Compare your answers to questions 5 and 6. Some features are common to most forms of electricity production, so it is worth remembering to include these in both your answers.

7   Renewable energy schemes are not always popular. Complete the table by giving a reason – economic, social or environmental – why people might not be in favour of a new hydro-electric dam in their area.

Issue	Reason
Economic	
Social	
Environmental	

8   How will the following changes affect the demand for energy?
    Tick the correct answer.

	Increase	Remain the same	Decrease
A change in employment types in a country from farming to industrial			
An increase in the use of energy-saving appliances			
A downturn in the world economy			
An increase in average household wages			
A warmer than expected winter temperature in a temperate country			
The building of a more affordable car in a low-income country (LIC)			
A law meaning power companies must use more renewable sources of energy			
An increase in population			

9   Table 2.2 shows an estimate of the annual power use in different countries.

Country	Energy use per person (kWh)
Angola	2791
Australia	63459
Bangladesh	2912
Belgium	53396
Burkina Faso	905
Cambodia	4035
India	7143
Japan	39985
Qatar	194222
United Arab Emirates	148577
United States of America	78754
Zambia	3419

Table 2.2: Annual energy use per person in selected countries.

a   Complete the two tables.

Greatest energy use per person:

Rank	Country
1	
2	
3	

Least energy use per person:

Rank	Country
10	
11	
12	

b   Describe the similarities between the countries using the least amount of energy per person.

....

....

c   Suggest reasons why the countries at the top of the ranking use so much energy per person.

....

....

....

....

TIP

When completing calculations, use the space available to show your working. Remember to check whether a question needs the calculation to be presented with a certain level of accuracy, such as the nearest whole number or to one decimal place or specified number of significant figures.

d   Calculate how many people from Burkina Faso could be supplied with the energy consumed by one person in Australia. Show your answer to the nearest whole number.

....

e   Suggest why the data used in table is expressed as energy used per person for this comparison.

....

....

> Managing energy resources

Exercise 2.6

KEY WORDS

non-renewable (finite): a natural resource that is being used up faster than it is being replaced so it will eventually run out

renewable: an item or resource that will not be used up or can be replaced; also referred to as a non-finite resource

green hydrogen: hydrogen produced from the splitting of water molecules

blue hydrogen: hydrogen produced from natural gas

1 Households have a responsibility to use energy efficiently. They can achieve this by reducing consumption and reducing energy waste. State **two** practical examples of each of these strategies.

Reduce energy consumption:

Example 1: ....

....

Example 2: ....

....

Reduce energy waste:

Example 1: ....

....

Example 2: ....

....

2   Figure 2.6 shows energy use in a government building.

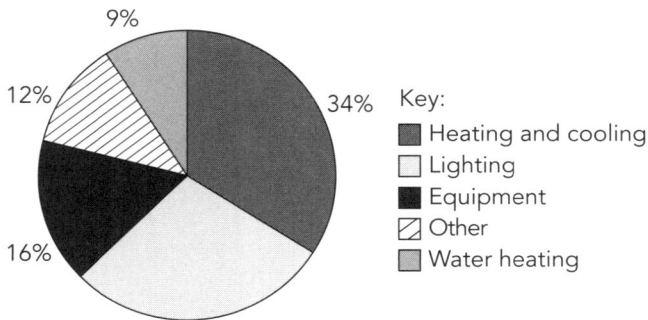

Figure 2.6: Proportions of energy use in a government building.

a   Calculate the percentage of energy used in lighting this government building.

....

...........................%

b   The energy use in the building costs US$120 000 per year.
Calculate the cost of the energy used to power the equipment.

....

US$...........................

c   It has been calculated that the offices in the building are wasting 9% of the
energy supplied to equipment because it is left in 'standby' mode when not in
use. Calculate the saving if staff switched off items when not in use.

....

US$...........................

d   Suggest **two** ways in which the building could be modified to reduce the
energy used in heating and cooling.

....

....

....

....

3 Many governments have agreed to increase the proportion of energy they produce from **renewable** sources. Suggest reasons why non-renewable resources are still likely to be needed for many years.

....

....

....

....

....

....

4 Scientists are developing energy systems that combust hydrogen as their fuel source.

a Suggest **one** benefit and **one** limitation of hydrogen combustion.

Benefit: ....

....

Limitation: ....

....

b Suggest **two** reasons why some scientists consider **green hydrogen** to be more sustainable than **blue hydrogen**.

Reason 1: ....

....

Reason 2: ....

....

5 Explain how the development of better battery technologies will reduce the need to exploit remaining fossil-fuel deposits.

....

....

....

....

6   A student plans to investigate the energy efficiency of three different types of light bulb.

   a   Outline the equipment and method they will need to use to complete this investigation.

   ....

   ....

   ....

   ....

   ....

   ....

   ....

   ....

   b   The information from this investigation can be used to calculate the cost of energy used by each type of light bulb. State the other factors that need to be considered when calculating the total costs of operating each type of light bulb.

   ....

   ....

   ....

   ....

> Fracking

Exercise 2.7

LEARNING INTENTIONS

In this exercise you will:

- describe the process of **fracking**
- evaluate the potential benefits and limitations of fracking.

KEY WORD

fracking: the common term for hydraulic fracking – the process of obtaining petroleum or natural gas from shale rock by the breaking open of rocks using water, sand and chemicals

1   Using Figure 2.7, describe the process of fracking to extract natural gas.

....

....

....

....

....

....

....

....

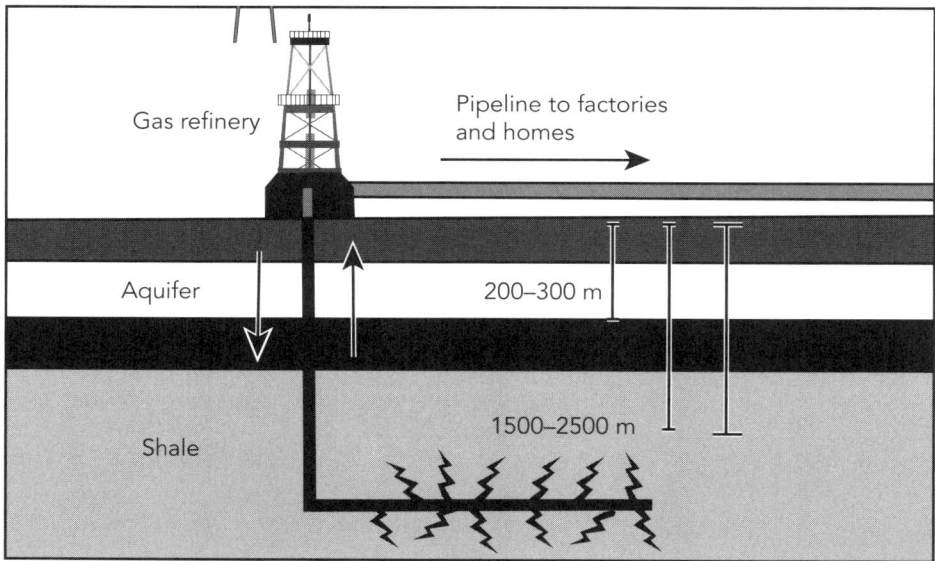

Figure 2.7: Simplified diagram of the fracking process for natural gas.

2   A plan has been submitted to allow the extraction of petroleum by fracking.

a   Suggest why people are concerned about fracking.

....

....

....

....

....

....

b   Suggest **two** benefits of the development of fracking to the local people in
     the area.

     Benefit 1: ....

     ....

     Benefit 2: ....

     ....

> Chapter 3

Land

> Soil components and crop growth

Exercise 3.1

LEARNING INTENTIONS

In this exercise you will:

- outline the components of soil
- categorise some characteristics of soil particles
- identify living organisms in soil
- apply knowledge from a soil-testing technique
- show your understanding of vocabulary relating to soils
- describe the effects of pore size on soils
- explain the properties of loam soil
- design an experiment to investigate root growth in different soil types
- apply knowledge of **photosynthesis** to a range of growing conditions.

KEY WORDS

photosynthesis: the process by which plants or plant-like organisms make food in the form of carbohydrate from carbon dioxide and water using energy from sunlight

erosion: the movement of rock and soil fragments to different locations

pH scale: a measure of the acidity or alkalinity of a substance such as the soil

weather: the day-to-day conditions of the atmosphere in a location

1   Use words from the list to complete the information about soil composition.

decrease   habitat   increase   mineral   organic

pores   weathering

Soil is a .... for plants and other organisms. The main components

of soil are: .... particles, the .... matter, living

organisms, gases and water. The proportion of gases in the soil will depend

on the size of the .... in the soil and the amount of water in

the soil at any particular time. In drought conditions, the volume of gases will

.... and water content .... The mineral particles

occupy the largest volume of the soil and are formed from the parent rocks by

.... and **erosion**.

2   Sort the following particles and their characteristics into the table below.
    Start with the **largest** particle.

Silt   <0.002 mm   silky

Sand   2.0–0.02 mm   sticky

Clay   0.02–0.002 mm   gritty

Particle	Size (mm)	Texture when moist

3   State **three** types of living organisms that are commonly found in soil.

a   ....

b   ....

c   ....

4   A student investigates the components of a soil by putting a sample in a jar,
    adding water, shaking it well and allowing it to settle.

    Explain what the student is likely to see after 15 minutes.

    ....

    ....

    ....

    ....

    ....

5   Answer the clues in this puzzle. When you have finished, the first initial of each
    answer will reveal the name of one of the three major nutrients needed by plants
    for successful growth in the first column.

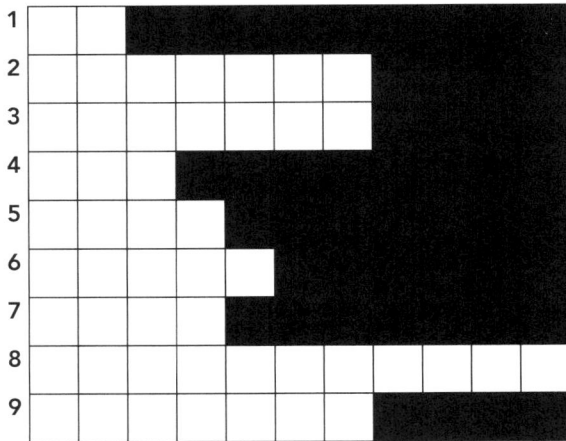

1   Scale on which the acidity of the soil is measured. (2)

2   Description of the part of the soil that is composed of the waste and remains
    of living organisms. (7)

3   Word to describe the feel of a soil. (7)

4   The main source of the gas found in the soil. (3)

5   The largest of the three mineral particle types. (4)

6   A word to describe the feel of silt particles when rubbed between your fingers. (5)

7   The name for the form of nutrients available for uptake by plants. (4)

8   What certain plant nutrients may become in the soil at the incorrect
    acidity levels. (11)

9   The component of the soil that is a combination of rock fragments and other
    non-living items. (7)

    Plant nutrient: ....

6   Complete the information about the impact of increasing pore size on soil
    characteristics. Tick the correct box.

    An increase in pore size in a soil will mean:

	Decreases	Increases	Remains the same
Drainage of water			
Soil **pH**			
Gas content			
Ease of cultivation			
Soil density			

7 What is loam soil?

....

....

8 Some students are investigating the impact that soil type has on the root growth of a type of soybean. They have been given the following equipment:

- Three soil types: a very sandy type; a soil with a high clay content; a loam soil
- Three soybeans
- Three identical glass jars.

a Using this equipment, design an investigation to investigate root growth of soybeans in different soil types.

....

....

....

....

....

....

....

....

b Suggest **three** improvements that could be made to make the results more reliable.

....

....

....

....

....

....

> **TIP**
>
> Read questions carefully, especially any words in bold. These words will be especially important when planning your answer.

9 Statements a–d name a plant and the conditions it is growing in.
For each one, name the factor that is limiting optimum photosynthesis.
Suggest a practical way in which it could be improved.

a A field of grain experiencing a period of drought.

Factor preventing optimum photosynthesis: ....

Practical way to improve: ....

....

....

....

b A crop of vegetables growing in a greenhouse when the **weather** has been cloudy for two weeks.

Factor preventing optimum photosynthesis: ....

Practical way to improve: ....

....

....

....

c A farmer planning to grow plants in an area with ice and snow on the ground.

Factor preventing optimum photosynthesis: ....

Practical way to improve: ....

....

....

....

d Plants grown in an artificially heated environment, in a country where days are short.

Factor preventing optimum photosynthesis: ....

Practical way to improve: ....

....

....

....

> Agriculture and crop yields

Exercise 3.2

KEY WORDS

agriculture: the cultivation of animals, plants and fungi for food and other products used to sustain human life

irrigation: the addition of water to a soil

leaching: the movement of a soluble chemical or mineral away from soil, usually caused by the action of rainwater

pesticide: a chemical used to control pests but also, less accurately, used as a collective term to describe pest- and disease-killing chemicals

pest: an animal that attacks or feeds on a plant

1   Draw lines to match the correct type of **agriculture** to its description.

Term	Description
arable farming	A farming system that both rears livestock and grows crops.
commercial farming	A farming system that only grows one type of crop.
intensive farming	A farming system that focuses on breeding and rearing livestock.
mixed farming	A farming system that produces large amounts from small areas of land.
monoculture	A farming system that supplies food for the farmers and their families.
pastoral farming	A farming system that focuses on the production of crops.
subsistence farming	A farming system where most of the food is sold to others.

2 Define the term 'sustainable food production'.

....

....

3 The trend in many countries is for agriculture to become more specialist, producing a small range of crops or animals compared to traditional systems, which produce a far wider range. Suggest why these changes have occurred.

....

....

....

....

....

....

> **TIP**
>
> For this question, you will need to apply your existing knowledge to a new situation. Consider what you know about the skills, processes and equipment needed to produce a crop or keep animals.

4 State **three** reasons why it is beneficial for farmers to increase the yield from their farms.

a ....

....

b ....

....

c ....

....

5 Table 3.1 shows an estimate of the amount of rice produced in China between 1960 and 2020.

Year	Rice production (million tonnes)
1960	60
1970	110
1980	140
1990	190
2000	190
2010	195
2020	215

Table 3.1: Rice production in China, 1960–2020.

a Plot the results as a bar chart.

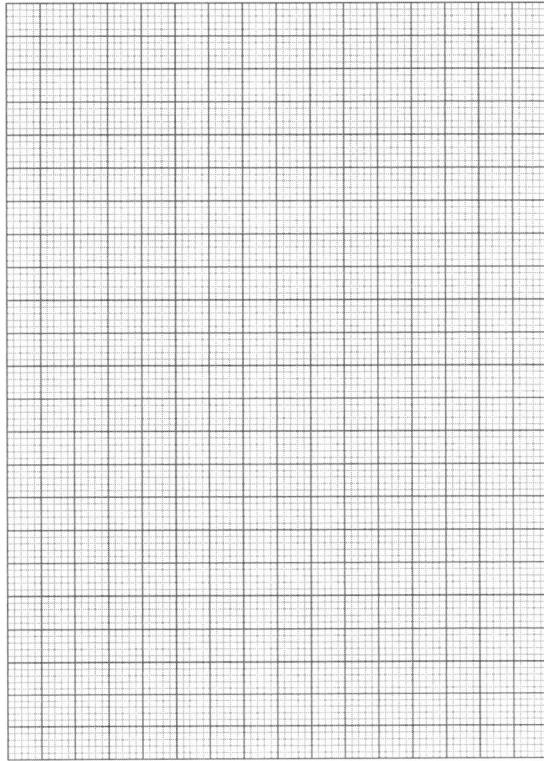

b Describe the trends in the graph.

....

....

....

....

....

....

c Suggest **two** reasons for the result recorded in 2000.

i ....

....

ii ....

....

d Calculate the percentage change in rice production in China between 1960 and 2020.

.... %

SELF-ASSESSMENT

How confident do you feel about drawing bar charts?
Tick the box that best describes your performance for each statement.

Feature	I forgot to add this feature	I added this feature but could do this better	I completed this feature well
I used a scale that used at least half the space available.			
I labelled the axes.			
I drew the bars using a ruler and pencil.			
I made the bars equal width.			
The bars do not touch each other.			
I plotted the bars correctly.			

If I could complete the activity again, I would pay more attention to:

....

....

6   Explain how the following techniques might be useful in increasing yield.

   a   Crop rotation

   ....

   ....

   ....

   ....

   b   Trickle/drip **irrigation**

   ....

   ....

   ....

   ....

   c   Genetically modified organisms

   ....

   ....

   ....

   ....

d Insecticides

....

....

....

....

e Herbicides

....

....

....

....

f Biological control of pests

....

....

....

....

g Agroforestry

....

....

....

....

7 Use the words in the list to complete sentences a–f. You may use each word once, more than once or not at all.

biodiversity   cotton   eutrophication   fertilisers   overcultivation

overgrazing   pesticides   pollution   resistance   resurgence

rice   salinisation   yield

a Food shortages may be a result of growing cash crops rather than food crops. An example of a cash crop is ....

b Mismanagement of irrigation may be a cause of soil erosion, ... and waterlogging.

c **Leaching** of nutrients into water sources is caused by overuse of ....

CAMBRIDGE IGCSE™ AND O LEVEL ENVIRONMENTAL MANAGEMENT: WORKBOOK

d Too much use of **pesticides** might result in **pest** .... – when the natural predators of the pest are also killed, allowing the pest population to increase again.

e The use of monoculture can result in a loss of .... as it reduces food sources and habitats for organisms.

f Keeping too much livestock on an area of land may result in the removal of natural vegetation due to ....

8 'It's impossible to feed the world without using unsustainable agricultural practices.' Do you agree with this statement? Justify your answer.

....

....

....

....

....

....

....

....

....

....

> The causes and impacts of soil erosion
Exercise 3.3

LEARNING INTENTIONS

In this exercise you will:

- interpret a map to describe patterns of soil degradation worldwide
- use information in a photograph to apply knowledge to an unfamiliar situation
- identify causes of soil erosion
- outline strategies to reduce soil erosion
- show understanding of how to increase organic matter in soil.

KEY WORD

humus: dark earth made of organic matter such as decayed leaves and plants

1   Scientists are concerned about the rate of soil erosion occurring worldwide. Research shows that it takes many years for soils to re-form in an area once it has been lost. Look at Figure 3.1, a map showing the status of the soil in different parts of the world.

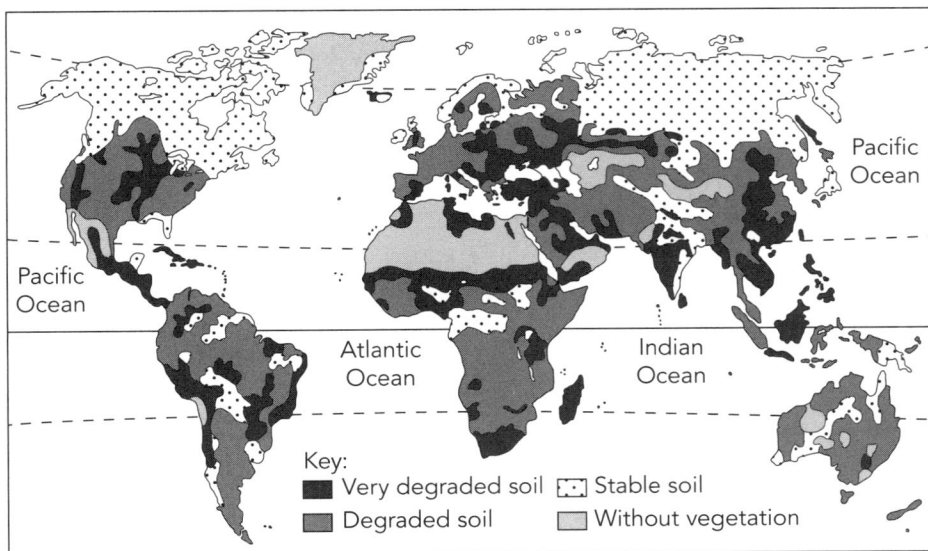

Figure 3.1: A map showing soil degradation worldwide.

a   Describe the degradation of soil shown on the map in Figure 3.1.

....

....

....

....

....

....

b   Suggest reasons for the location of the main areas which are marked as having 'stable soil'.

....

....

....

....

2   Figure 3.2 is a photograph showing the impact of erosion to a field caused by excessive water flow.

Figure 3.2: Soil erosion caused by the flow of water.

Describe the impacts of this soil erosion in the field and further downstream.

Impacts in the field: ....

....

....

....

Impacts downstream: ....

....

....

....

3 Excess water is only one cause of soil erosion. Complete the spider diagram to show other reasons for this type of erosion.

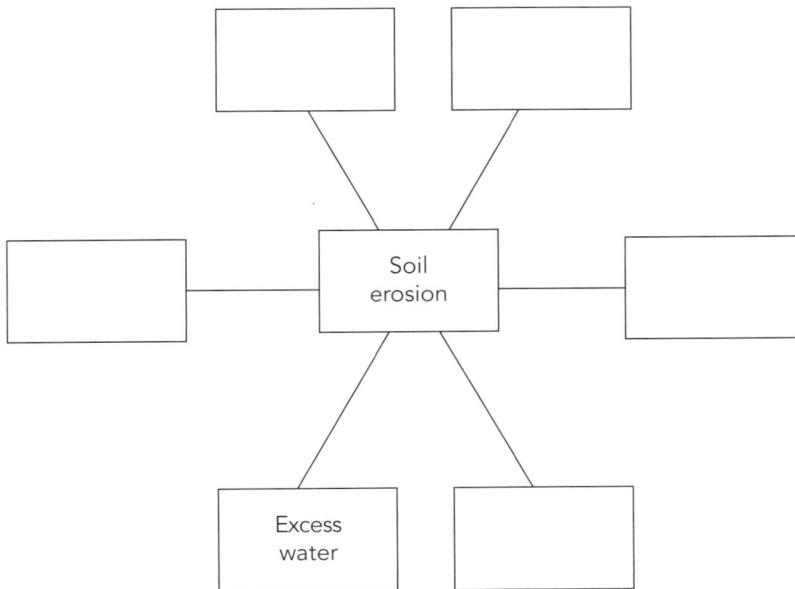

4 One method of reducing the risk of soil erosion is to increase the amount of organic matter in soil. This helps to improve the health and quality of the soil by the addition of **humus**, which helps stabilise smaller soil particles and acts like a sponge to hold additional water.

Circle the items in the list that will add organic matter to a soil.

animal manure   clay   composted plant material

food waste   dead leaves   recycled paper   sand

chalk   rocks

5 Use the words listed below to complete the information about techniques to reduce the risk of soil erosion. The words may be used once, more than once or not at all.

terracing   infiltrate   yield   topsoil   contours   bunds

roots   evaporate   famine   permeable

Farmers need to cultivate land efficiently if they are to maximise its yield.

If the techniques they use result in the loss of the ...., fertility

is lost. One way in which the impact of erosion on a steep slope may be reduced

is by .... This reduces the speed of the water and allows it to

.... the soil. Contour ploughing works on a similar principle,

the ridges and troughs following the .... of the land. The use of

.... – artificial banks at the edges of growing spaces – also helps to

hold back water.

Wind erosion may also be reduced by planting natural vegetation as wind breaks

at the edges of fields. These act as .... barriers that reduce the

speed of the wind.

There are numerous other ways of helping to reduce erosion. Leaving soil

covered with the vegetation from a crop, for example, means that soil is retained

by the .... of the plants. Bare soil increases the risk of erosion.

Lack of topsoil may increase the risk of desertification in an area, increasing

.... and malnutrition in the local population.

> Chapter 4
Water

> Water sources

Exercise 4.1

KEY WORD

aquifer: water that is stored in porous rocks under the ground

condensation: the process in which water vapour turns in to liquid water – the opposite of evaporation

1   Use the words in the box to fill in the gaps in sentences a–d.

    evaporation   surface run-off   infiltration   intercepted

    a   Some rainfall does not reach the ground because it is .... by trees and plants.

    b   Some rainfall flows over the surface and ends up in streams and rivers. This is called ....

    c   Some rainfall re-enters the atmosphere in a process called ....

    d   Some rainfall seeps into the ground, which is called ....

2 Look at Figure 4.1, which shows the water cycle.

Figure 4.1: The water cycle.

   a Write the correct names next to the three arrows to show the processes in the water cycle.

   b Add labels and arrows to the figure to show:

      run-off   **interception**   **condensation**

3 Explain how run-off might change if an area of forested land was developed to create a hotel complex.

....

....

....

....

4 Look at descriptions a–e. Fill in each gap with the name of the correct ocean from the list.

   Atlantic   **Pacific**   **Indian**   **Arctic**   **Southern**

   a The .... Ocean encircles the Antarctic.

   b The .... Ocean has North America to its west and north, and Europe and Africa to the east. South America lies to its south.

   c The .... Ocean is the most northerly of the five main oceans.

d The .... Ocean is located between Africa and Australia.

e The .... Ocean is the largest of the main oceans. It is located between Asia and Australia to the west and the Americas to the east.

5 Name **two** rock types that could accumulate water in an aquifer.

....

....

> The availability of water on Earth

Exercise 4.2

1 There are 1.4 billion km^3 of water on Earth, but only 3% is fresh water – the rest is saline. Calculate how many cubic kilometres of Earth's water is saline. Show your working.

....

....

2 There are about 13 000 km^3 of water, in the form of water vapour, in Earth's atmosphere. Calculate the percentage of Earth's water that this represents, using the figure for the total water on Earth from Exercise 1. Show your working.

....

....

3 Suggest a source of water for a low-income country (LIC) that has very low rainfall.

....

....

4 The table shows the water usage in India, by percentage for each category. Complete the table, pie chart and key.

Type of water usage	Percentage (%)
irrigation	68
domestic	7
industry	

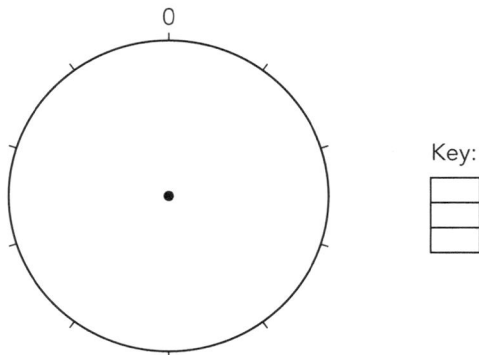

0

Key:

5 Potable water can be obtained by distilling salt water. Complete the description of the distillation process using the words in the list.

condenses   **vapour**   **heated**   **cools**

Salt water is ...., causing water .... to be given off.

This then forms pure liquid water as it ....

6 An environmental scientist says that reverse osmosis is a more sustainable method of obtaining drinking water from the sea than distillation. How far do you agree with this opinion?

....

....

....

....

....

....

....

....

7 Suggest **three** purposes of a multipurpose dam project.

a ....

....

b ....

....

c ....

....

8 Figure 4.2 shows the location of a large dam. Suggest why this is a good site for a dam.

....

....

....

....

....

....

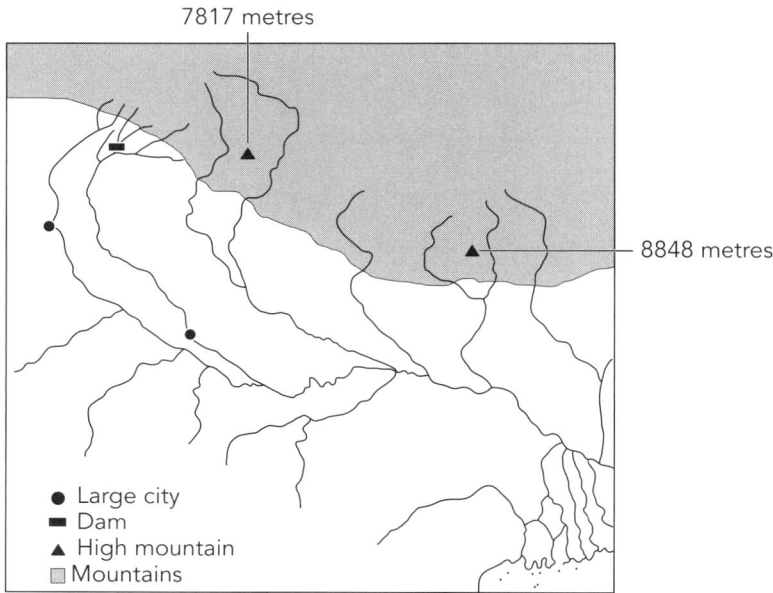

Figure 4.2: A map showing the location of a dam.

> Water pollution

Exercise 4.3

LEARNING INTENTIONS

In this exercise you will:

- define some key terminology
- show your understanding of eutrophication
- describe the effect on ecosystems and human health of industrial waste
- explain how water is treated to improve its quality
- describe the effects of **acid rain** on water bodies
- plan an investigation into the impacts of **nutrient enrichment** in water.

KEY WORDS

acid rain: rain that has been made more acidic by the presence of sulfur dioxide and oxides of nitrogen

nutrient enrichment: an increase in the level of nutrients in a habitat or ecosystem

algae: plant-like, photosynthetic organisms that lack true stems, roots and leaves

1 Write a brief definition of the following term:

Sewage wastewater: ....

2 Write the following numbered statements in the correct order in the flow chart to show the process of eutrophication.

1 **algae** die

2 oxygen used up and level lowered

3 stimulate algal growth (**algal bloom**)

4 fish and other aquatic creatures die

5 nutrients enter water

6 bacteria decompose dead algae

> **KEY WORD**
>
> **algal bloom:** the rapid growth of algae in water, caused particularly by a surge of nutrients

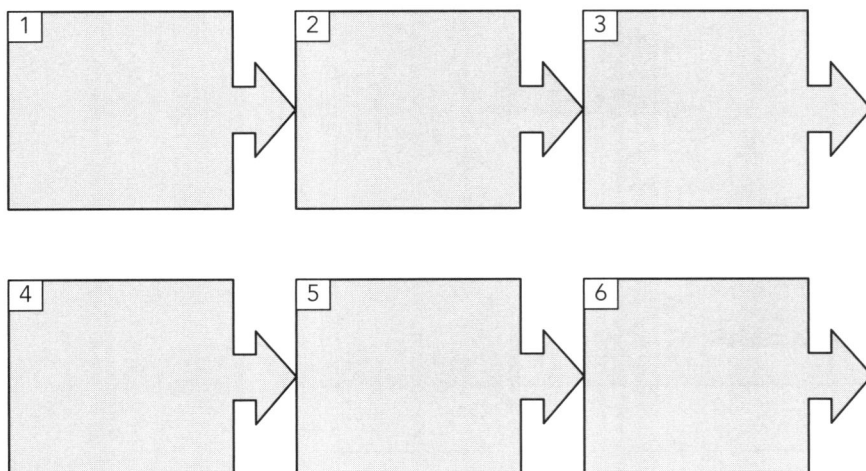

3 A new chemical factory was set up on a river (see Figure 4.3). Several years later, it was noticed that fish were dying in the river downstream of the factory. People in a local village relied on the river for fish. The water was tested and found to contain mercury.

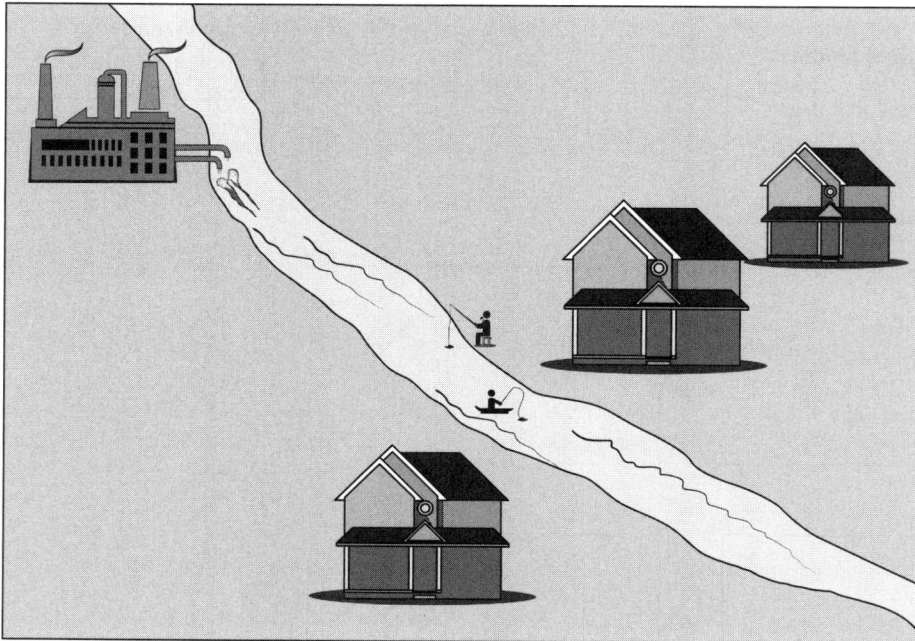

Figure 4.3: A chemical factory located on a river.

a Explain why it took several years for the fish to start dying.

....

....

....

b Suggest the risks to human health caused by this factory.

....

....

....

4 Use the words below to complete this paragraph about sewage treatment.
You may need to use some words more than once.

> chlorine   bacteria   organic   treatment   larger   oxygen

Sewage is treated to reduce the amount of .... material. If this is

not done before the sewage is sent to a river, then .... will break

it down, producing a biological .... demand. To make river water

potable, it is passed through a water .... plant. The water is filtered

to remove .... particles. It is disinfected with ....

to kill ....

5 Acid rain is caused by the release of oxides of sulfur and nitrogen into the atmosphere. As this acidified rain flows through the soil it can leach out metals such as aluminium and mercury which then move into water bodies such as rivers and lakes.

These metals are toxic to aquatic organisms. Explain two ways that these metals can affect the whole of a food chain.

....

....

....

....

6 It was noticed that the community of animals and plants in two small lakes, which were quite close together, were very different. It was suggested that this might be due to differences in the nutrients in the lake.

Plan an investigation that could be used to compare the effects of nutrient enrichment with nitrate on these two different bodies of water.

....

....

....

....

....

....

PEER ASSESSMENT

When you have planned your investigation, swap plans with a partner. How easy would it be to follow their description? Is there enough detail to carry out the investigation? Are there any missing details?

Give your partner feedback on how well they have done by writing a report based on these questions.

Read their assessment of your own plan and then modify it in response to their feedback.

> Water-related diseases

Exercise 4.4

LEARNING INTENTIONS

In this exercise you will:

- describe how malaria is transmitted

- identify strategies for controlling malaria and cholera.

KEY WORD

vector: an organism that carries a disease-producing organism

1 Name the **vector** that carries malaria and explain why the disease is common in areas where rice is grown.

Vector: ....

Reason: ....

....

....

....

2 Look at the following strategies for controlling water-related diseases. For each strategy, tick whether it would be effective at controlling malaria or cholera.

Strategy	Malaria	Cholera
Sleeping under a net		
Boiling water before drinking it		
Vaccination		
Covering the surface of water with a layer of oil		
Washing your hands		
Using insect repellent		
Chlorinating water		
Sterilising targeted insects		

TIP

Remember that malaria is not a bacterial disease and, as such, it cannot be transmitted from person to person nor from drinking contaminated water.

> Exploiting marine species
Exercise 4.5

LEARNING INTENTIONS

In this exercise you will:

- show your understanding of **bycatch**
- explain some of the issues surrounding overfishing
- calculate the effect of overfishing on a species.

KEY WORD

bycatch: animals caught by fishers that are not the intended target of the fishing effort

1 Name **three** types of bycatch.

....

2 List **three** possible reasons for overfishing.

a ....

b ....

c ....

3   Look at Figure 4.4. Use the information to calculate the percentage decrease in the mass of cod between the 1930s and the 2000s.

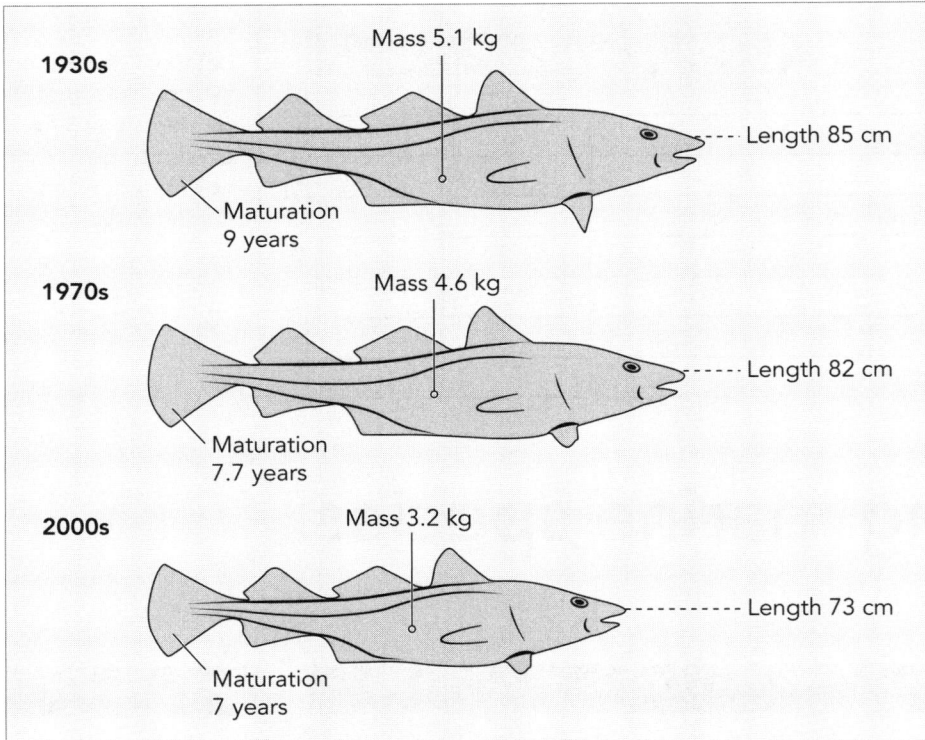

1930s
Mass 5.1 kg
Length 85 cm
Maturation 9 years

1970s
Mass 4.6 kg
Length 82 cm
Maturation 7.7 years

2000s
Mass 3.2 kg
Length 73 cm
Maturation 7 years

Figure 4.4: Statistics on cod in the 1930s, 1970s and 2000s.

....

....

....

> Managing marine species and marine aquaculture

Exercise 4.6

1   Solve the clues to complete the puzzle grid.

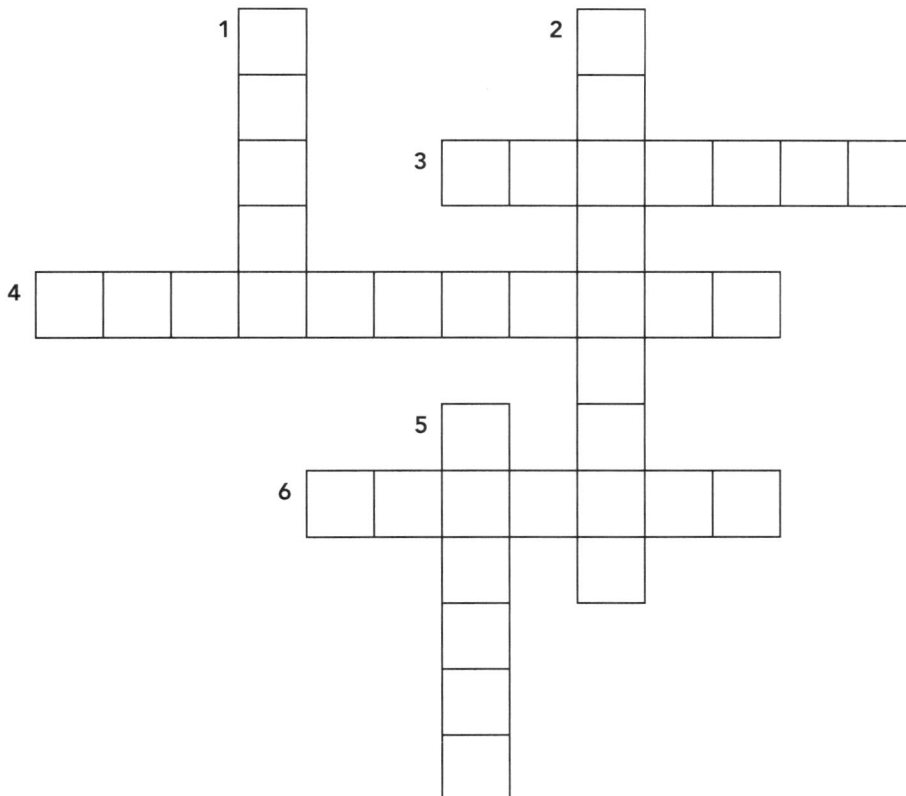

Across

3   The .... is when the non-intended species or ones that are too small are caught. (7)

4   .... is the cultivation of organisms under controlled, semi-natural conditions. (11)

6   Closed .... are times of the year when fishing for certain species is banned. (7)

Down

1   The legal limit on the amount of fish that can be caught is the .... (5)

2   A country's responsibility to manage its fisheries operates within the economic .... zone. (9)

5   The intended species of harvesting is the .... species. (6)

2   Name **three** types of marine organism that can be cultivated using marine aquaculture.

a   ....

b   ....

c   ....

3   Give **one** reason why it is difficult to farm marine fish as food.

....

....

....

4   The sea cucumber is a slow-moving animal that lives on the seabed and feeds on small organic particles. In 1991, people began fishing for the sea cucumber around the Galapagos Islands in the Pacific Ocean to the west of Ecuador. However, the fishery had many problems and the Ecuadorian government banned it in 1992. Some fishing happened in 1994, but the ban was reimposed. When the fishery reopened in 1999, the government required surveys to be carried out every year, both before and after the fishing season. The data collected was the number of individual sea cucumbers in a defined area.

a   Write a plan for a survey that could be carried out every year before the fishing season and again after the fishing season.

....

....

....

....

....

....

....

....

The results of these surveys, between 1999 and 2005, are shown in the graph.

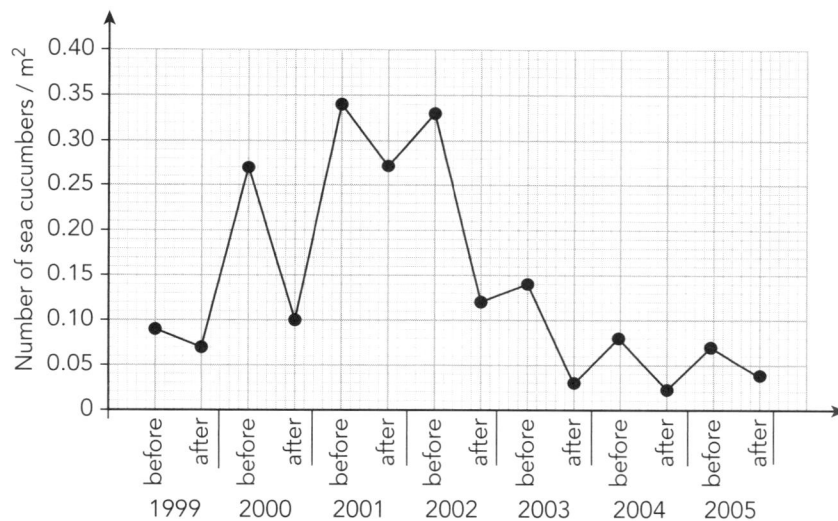

Figure 4.5: The results of a survey measuring the number of sea cucumbers in 1m².

b   In what year did the recorded number of sea cucumbers in m² decrease the most? Calculate the size of the decrease.

....

....

c   Describe and explain the patterns shown by these results.

....

....

....

d Do you think there are any trends in the data? Explain your answer.

....

....

....

5 **a** In order to take pressure off the natural population, investigations are being carried out into the possibility of culturing sea cucumbers.

In one experiment, sea cucumbers were kept in tanks of seawater and fed with different food. Some young sea cucumbers weighing 0.8 g were placed into two separate tanks which had seawater flowing through them. The sea cucumbers were fed with different diets in the two tanks. In tank A they were fed chicken manure and in tank B they were fed with shrimp starter as food. The sea cucumbers were weighed every 15 days for 45 days. The arrangement of the tanks is shown in the diagram.

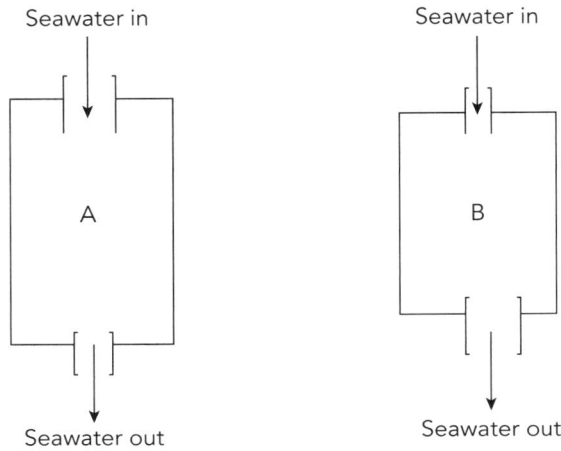

Figure 4.6: The arrangement of tanks in an experiment to culture sea cucumbers.

Using all the information and the diagram, together with your own knowledge, identify **two** limitations in this experiment. Suggest how it could be improved.

Limitation 1: ....

Limitation 2: ....

Suggestions for improvement: ....

....

....

....

....

....

b   The results from the experiment described are shown in the graph.

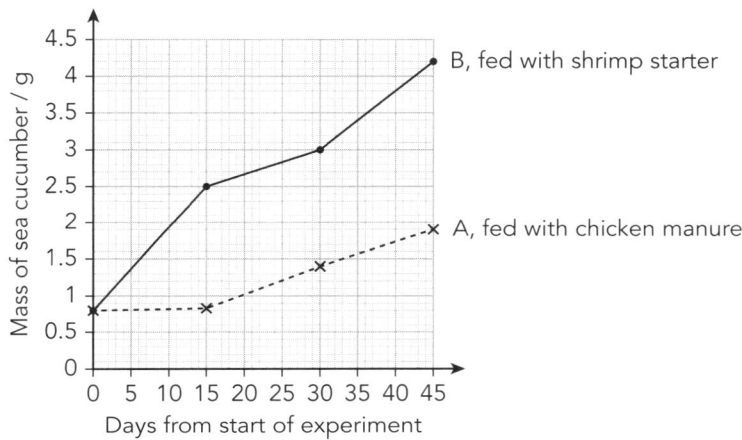

Figure 4.7: The results of the experiment to culture sea cucumbers.

Compare the trend in the data for the two graphs.

....

....

....

....

....

› Oil pollution in the oceans

Exercise 4.7

1   Solve the across clues to complete the puzzle. Each question relates to an aspect of oil pollution. When the puzzle is complete, the first initial of each answer will reveal the name of a famous oil spill.

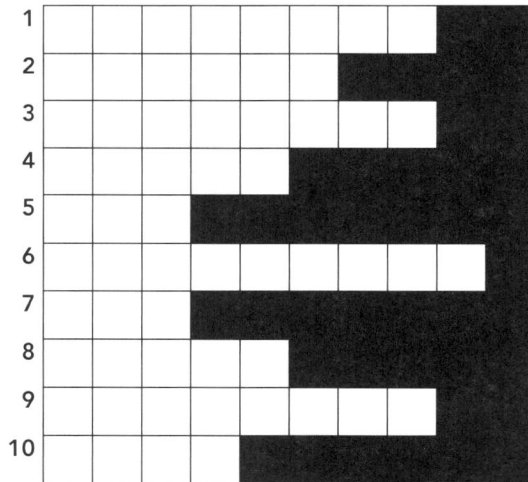

1 Unintended or unexpected incident. (8)

2 The sea environment. (6)

3 Location of many oil rigs. (8)

4 Name to describe unrefined oil. (5)

5 Liquid fossil fuel. (3)

6 The reason for many oil-tanker spills. (9)

7 Excluded from the sea when the sea is covered in oil. (3)

8 The impact of an oil spill on many organisms. (5)

9 An oil spill will severely affect a local tourism _____. (8)

10 The ideal number of oil spills. (4)

Name of incident: ....

2 Explain why onshore oil spills have a far smaller impact than those that occur in the sea.

....

....

....

....

3 State **three** ways in which an oil spill may be cleared up. Give the advantages and disadvantages for each method.

Method	Advantage	Disadvantage

4 Figure 4.8 shows major oil spills from 1967 to 2024.

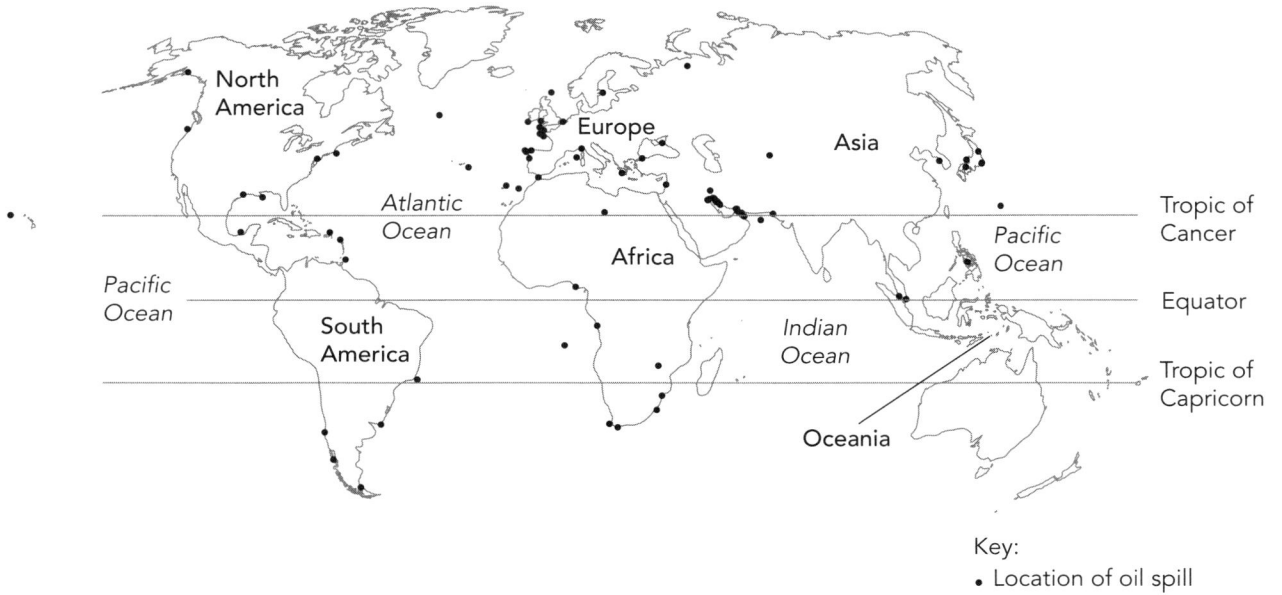

Figure 4.8: The location of major oil spills, 1967–2024.

a Describe the distribution of marine oil spills around the world from 1967 to 2024.

....

....

....

....

....

....

....

....

b Suggest **five** ways in which marine oil spills may affect marine life.

i ....

....

ii ....

....

iii ....

....

iv ....

....

v ....

....

5 Figure 4.9 shows the number of oil transport movements between 1970 and 2014, and the number of major oil spills during the same period.

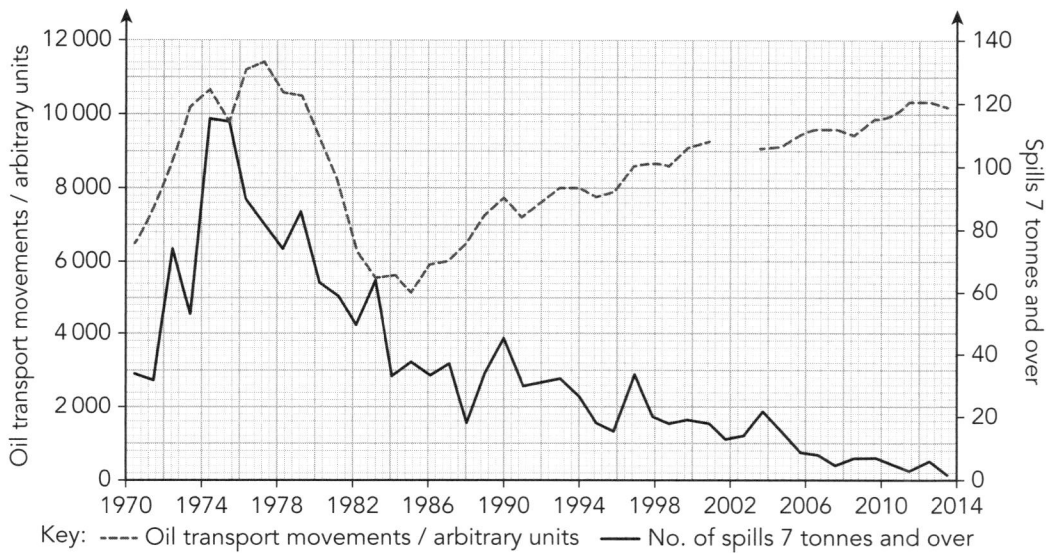

Figure 4.9: Oil transport movements and oil spills, 1970–2014.
[Sources: Fearnresearch 1970–1989, Lloyds List Intelligence 1990–2014]

a Complete the graph by plotting the data for the seaborne oil trade for 2002: 7800 transport movements / arbitrary units.

b In which year was there the greatest number of major oil spills?

....

c Describe the trends in the amount of oil transport movements taking place.

....

....

....

....

d What changes to tanker design might be responsible for the trend in major oil spills?

....

....

....

....

6 In 1983, the MARPOL treaty was introduced. This has helped to reduce the number of major oil spills. Explain why the drop in incidents after the treaty was gradual rather than immediate.

....

....

....

....

> Plastic pollution in the oceans

Exercise 4.8

LEARNING INTENTIONS

In this exercise you will:

* describe different types of plastic

* identify strategies to reduce plastic pollution and explain how they could be implemented.

1 Use the words in the list to complete the information about types of plastic.

biodegradable   **fossil fuel**   **microorganisms**   **5 mm**

starch   **microplastics**

Plastics exist in many different types. Some can be broken down by

.... and are called .... The first types of

plastic were non-biodegradable and relied on the .... industry.

Some plastics are less than .... in length and are called

.... Some bioplastics are made from biological raw materials

such as ....

2 There are many initiatives being developed to reduce plastic pollution.
Describe **three** such ideas and how they could be achieved.

a   ....

    ....

b   ....

    ....

c   ....

    ....

3 Albatrosses (large sea birds) catch fish from the surface of the sea.
They often mistake plastic pieces floating on the sea for fish. The albatrosses
feed the plastic to their chicks, who make them into a pellet and eject (egest)
them from their stomach.

Suggest how the ingestion of plastic pieces might affect the albatross chicks.

....

....

....

....

---

4 The extent of the problem in question 3 can be assessed by collecting the egested pellets and searching through them for plastic pieces. In one study, ten pellets showed an average of 72 pieces of plastic per pellet with an average mass per pellet of 37 g.

a Calculate the average mass of a single piece of plastic. Give your answer to two decimal places.

....

....

b These data were compared with data from another location using a bar chart.

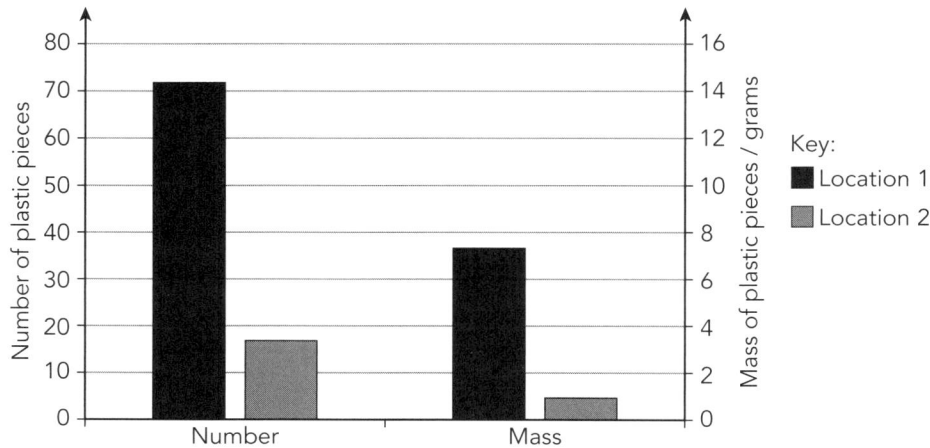

Figure 4.10: A comparison of the mass and numbers of pieces of plastic in egested pellets from albatross chicks at two locations.

Suggest three factors that might explain the difference in the quantity of plastic appearing in the egested pellets between locations 1 and 2.

i ....

....

ii ....

....

iii ....

....

Chapter 5

The atmosphere and human activities

> The composition and structure of the atmosphere

Exercise 5.1

LEARNING INTENTIONS
In this exercise you will:
• show your understanding of the composition of the atmosphere
• complete a diagram of the structure of the atmosphere.

KEY WORDS
ultraviolet radiation: harmful rays from the Sun
respiration: the process by which living things release energy from food to carry out the processes of life, such as movement

1 Read sentences A, B and C about the composition of the atmosphere. Which ones are correct? Tick **one** answer.

A Nitrogen and carbon dioxide make up most of the atmosphere.

B Carbon dioxide is called a variable gas because its quantity can change.

C The atmosphere is only made up of gases.

A only ☐

B only ☐

C only ☐

A and B ☐

B and C ☐

None of the above ☐

2 Complete the table using the appropriate letter from the list.
There are ten possibilities. Use each letter only once.

A	Oxygen	**F**	Sulfur dioxide
B	Carbon dioxide	**G**	Water vapour
C	Helium	**H**	Argon
D	Ozone	**I**	Methane
E	Nitrogen	**J**	Krypton

Statement	Letter
This gas is used by plants in photosynthesis	
Ultraviolet radiation is absorbed by this gas	
The most abundant gas in the atmosphere and a product of volcanic eruptions	
This gas is produced by photosynthesis and is used in **respiration**	
Keeping livestock can increase levels of this gas	

3 The diagram below shows the structure of the atmosphere.
Complete the diagram using words from the list.

mesosphere   thermosphere   stratopause   temperature inversion

temperature   tropopause   pressure   stratosphere

mesopause   troposphere

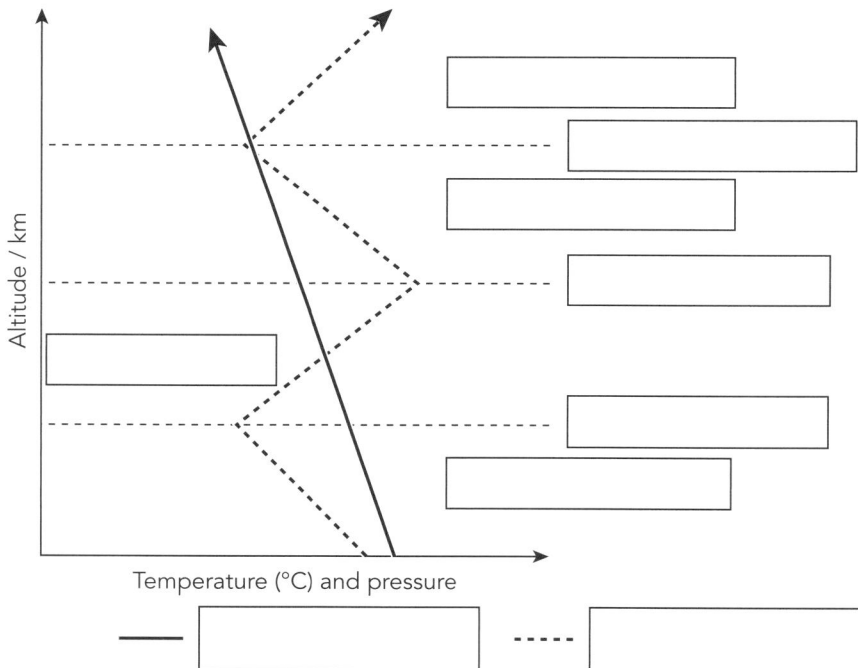

> The greenhouse effect and climate change

Exercise 5.2

<table>
<tr><td>

LEARNING INTENTIONS

In this exercise you will:

* describe the natural greenhouse effect

* interpret data about **greenhouse gases**

* explore the link between carbon dioxide and global temperatures

* explain the causes of increased greenhouses gases in the atmosphere

* analyse data about carbon dioxide emissions

* consider the impacts of **climate** change

* name some strategies to deal with the impacts of climate change.

</td><td>

KEY WORDS

greenhouse gas: a gas that absorbs radiation and emits the energy as thermal or heat energy, such as carbon dioxide, methane, nitrous oxides and water vapour

climate: the weather conditions in a location based on the weather over many years

enhanced greenhouse effect: when human activities increase the warming effect of the natural greenhouse effect

</td></tr>
</table>

1   Use words from the list to complete the sentences about the natural greenhouse effect. Each word may be used once, more than once or not at all.

nitrogen   short-wave   absorbed   long-wave   carbon dioxide   emitted

Radiation from the Sun is called .... (or solar) radiation.

Almost half of this radiation is .... by Earth's surface and makes

Earth warmer. .... radiation is .... by Earth.

This radiation is .... by greenhouses gases such as

.... and the atmosphere heats up.

2   Research has shown that the major greenhouse gases are increasing in concentration in the atmosphere. Study Table 5.1, which contains information about three greenhouse gases in 2021.

Greenhouse gas	Concentration in 2021 (ppm)	Concentration in ppm in 1750 (pre-industrial times)	% increase since pre-industrial times	Lifespan in atmosphere (years)
Carbon dioxide	417.00	227.00		100s–1000s of years
Methane	1.92	0.73		12
Nitrous oxides	0.33	0.27		114

Table 5.1: Greenhouse gases.

    a   Which greenhouse gas in the table had the highest concentration in 2021?

        ....

    b   Complete the % increase since pre-industrial times for carbon dioxide, methane and nitrous oxides.

    c   Referring to the data in the table only, explain why scientists are particularly concerned about rising levels of carbon dioxide as a greenhouse gas.

        ....

        ....

        ....

3   Figure 5.1 shows two graphs – changes in the concentration of carbon dioxide in the atmosphere and global average surface temperatures.

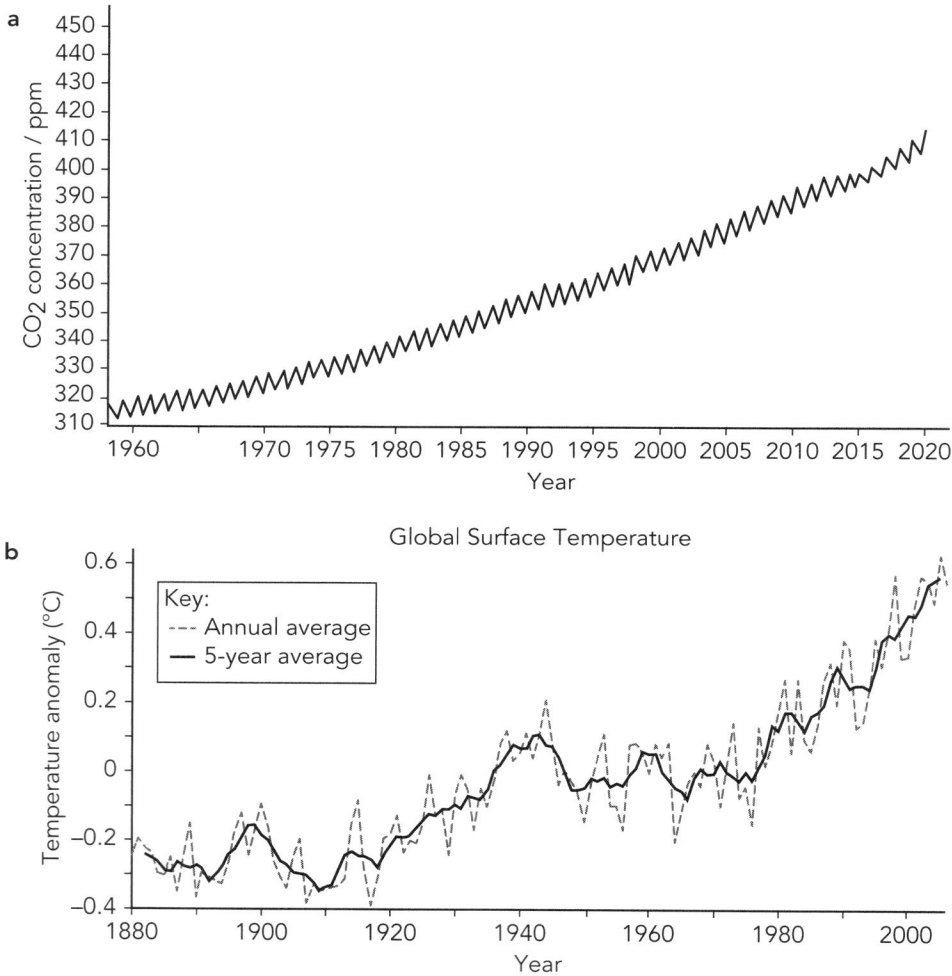

Figure 5.1: **a** The concentration of carbon dioxide in the atmosphere; **b** global average surface temperatures.

a Describe the relationship between the concentration of carbon dioxide and global average surface temperatures, using evidence from the graphs.

....

....

....

....

b Look again at graph a, showing carbon dioxide concentration. Suggest why carbon dioxide concentration fluctuates during the year. (Hint: think about how carbon dioxide is produced.)

....

....

4 Explain why an increase in carbon dioxide concentration can lead to a change in the temperature of the atmosphere.

....

....

5 Table 5.2 shows global carbon dioxide emissions by sector in 2022.

Sector	% of total emissions
Residential	10
Transport	21
Industry	29
Electricity generation	39
Other	1

Table 5.2: Carbon dioxide emissions by sector, 2022.

a Using the information in the table, complete the pie chart and key below.

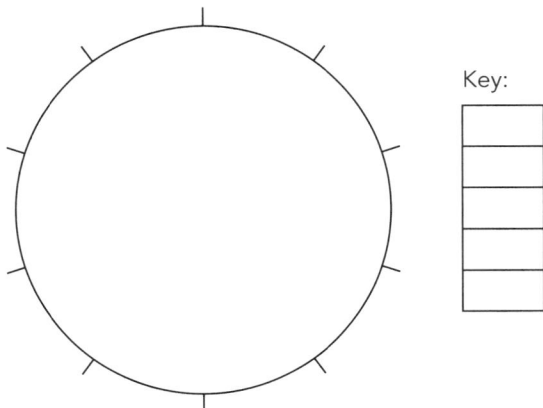

Key:

b Which **two** sectors combined generated just over two-thirds of global carbon dioxide emissions in 2022? Circle the correct answer from the options below.

transport and industry   **electricity generation and industry**

transport and electricity generation   **transport and residential**

6 Table 5.3 shows carbon dioxide emissions (from the burning of fossils fuels and cement production) per capita for selected countries between 2002 and 2022. The world average was 4.9 tonnes of CO_2 per person in 2022.

	Carbon emissions per capita (tonnes of CO_2)					
	2002	2006	2010	2014	2018	2022
World	4.1	4.7	4.8	4.9	4.6	5.0
China HIC	2.9	4.9	6.2	7.1	7.0	8.7
USA HIC	19.6	19.1	17.5	17.0	17.0	15.0
UK HIC	8.9	8.9	7.8	6.7	8.0	7.0
India LIC	1.1	1.3	1.6	2.0	2.0	2.0
Kenya LIC	0.2	0.3	0.3	0.3	0.4	1.0
Bangladesh LIC	0.2	0.3	0.4	0.4	0.6	1.0

Table 5.3: Carbon dioxide emissions per capita for selected countries, 2002–2022.

a Plot line graphs to show the data in the table on the grid below. Include a key. The world average has already been plotted.

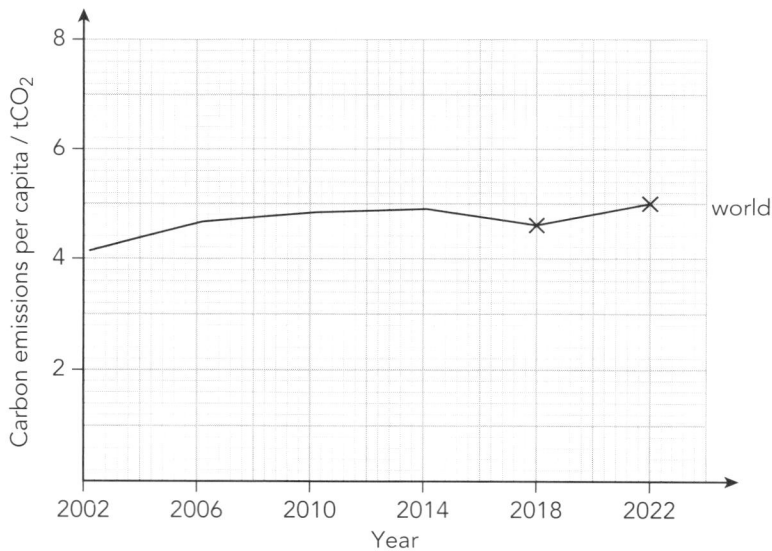

b   Using evidence from the line graph, describe the difference in the carbon dioxide emissions per capita between high-income countries (HICs) and low-income countries (LICs) between 2002 and 2022.

....

....

....

....

....

....

c   How many times greater were the carbon dioxide emissions per capita from the USA than from India in 2022? Circle the correct answer.

   8 times   4 times   9 times   7.5 times   6 times   7 times

d   How many countries on the line graph were above the world average in 2022?

....

....

....

e   Suggest reasons for the difference you noted in part b.

....

....

....

....

....

....

7 Figure 5.2 shows the possible impacts of global warming as a result of an increase in carbon dioxide emissions and the **enhanced greenhouse effect**.

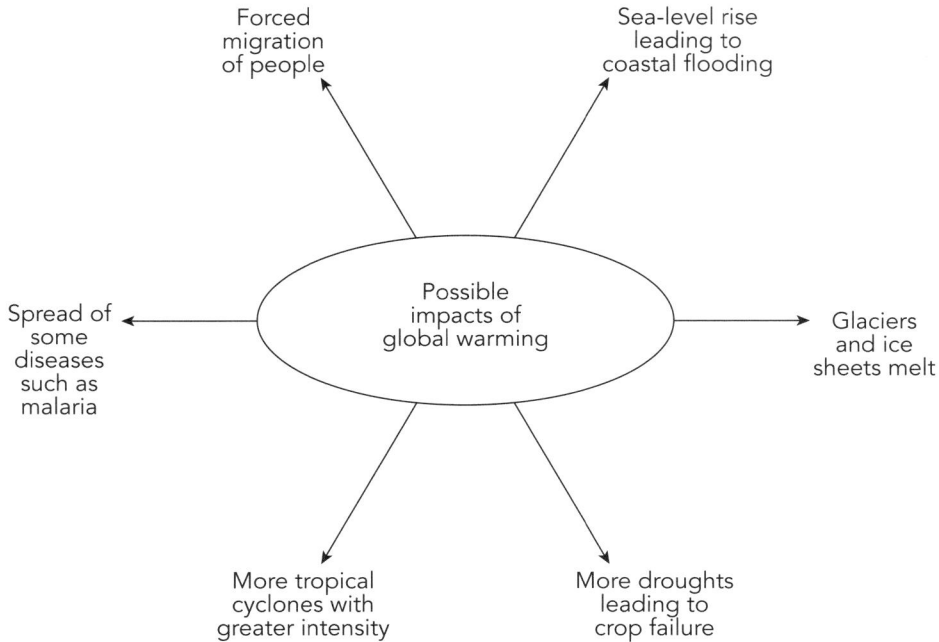

Figure 5.2: Possible impacts of global warming through increased carbon dioxide emissions.

Suggest reasons why governments in countries such as Bangladesh – which is not a major carbon dioxide emitter – are more concerned about global warming than other countries.

....

....

....

....

....

....

8 Name **two** mitigation strategies and **two** adaptation strategies for dealing with the impacts of climate change.

   a Mitigation strategies:

      i ....

      ii ....

b   Adaptation strategies:

i   ....

ii   ....

SELF-ASSESSMENT

Having completed this section, fill in the T chart to show the things you were confident that you knew and the questions that you struggled with or did not feel confident about. Reflect on how you could reduce the right-hand list.

Confident	Not confident

〉 Acid rain

Exercise 5.3

LEARNING INTENTIONS

In this exercise you will:

- show the process of how **acid rain** is formed
- analyse a graph about sulfur-dioxide emissions
- practise drawing a divided bar chart
- interpret data on sulfur-dioxide concentrations
- evaluate an investigation into sulfur-dioxide emissions.

KEY WORD

acid rain: rain that has been made more acidic by the presence of sulfur dioxide and oxides of nitrogen

1 Using the statements below, complete the flow chart to show the cause of acid rain. The statements are not in the correct order.

falls to Earth as acid rain

sulfur dioxide and nitrogen oxides released

dry deposition

gases mix with water vapour and oxygen in the atmosphere

blown by winds over large distances

weak solution of nitric and sulfuric acids produced

1 Fossil fuels burnt in power stations and transport	2	3	4

5	6	7	8 Wet deposition

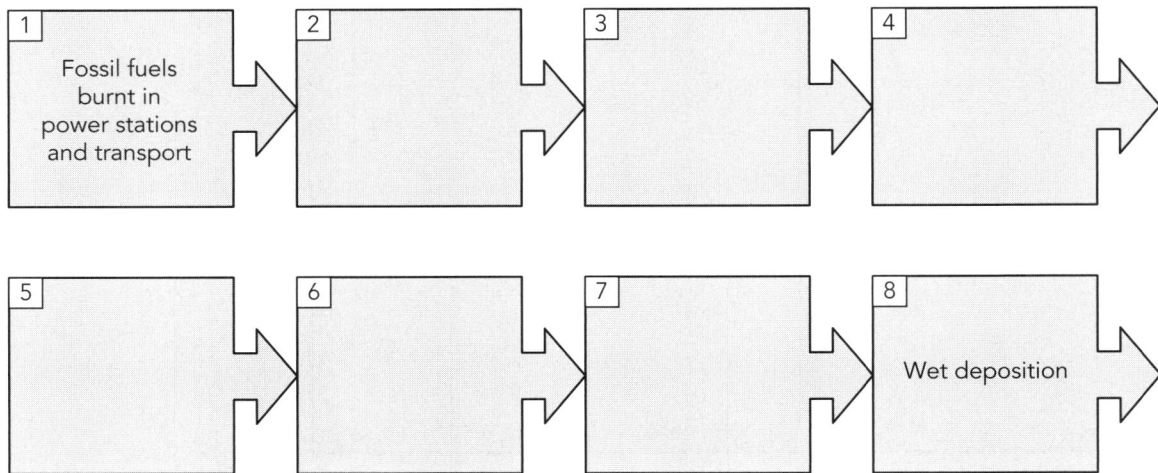

2 Name **one** way in which the impacts of acid rain can be managed. For your chosen strategy, explain one limitation.

Strategy: ....

Limitation: ....

....

3   Look at Figure 5.3, a divided bar chart showing sources of sulfur-dioxide emissions in India in 2021.

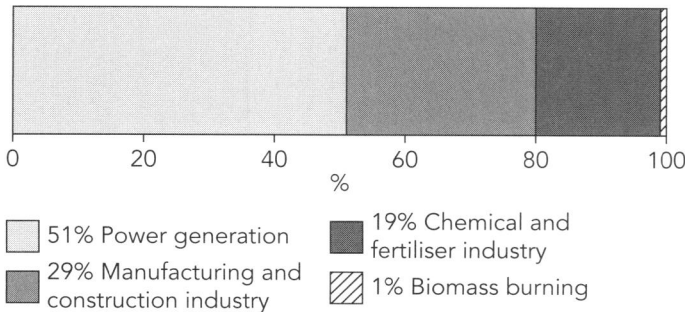

51% Power generation

29% Manufacturing and construction industry

19% Chemical and fertiliser industry

1% Biomass burning

Figure 5.3: Sulfur-dioxide emissions in India, 2021.

Which source produced the highest sulfur-dioxide emissions in 2021?

....

4   Table 5.4 shows the percentage of nitrogen oxide emitted by sources in India in 2021.

Source of nitrogen oxide	%
Agriculture	92
Burning of waste	6
Industry	1
Land use change and deforestation	0.6
Power generation	0.4

Table 5.4: Sources of nitrogen oxide emissions in India, 2021.

Use the data in the table to complete a divided bar chart on the grid to show the sources of nitrogen oxide emissions in India in 2021.

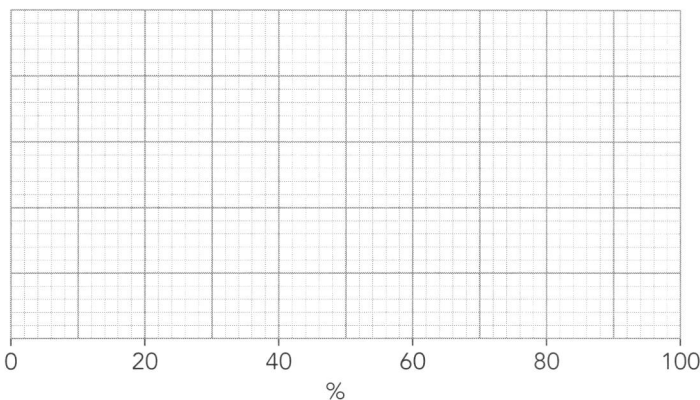

Key:

☐ Agriculture   ☐ Burning of waste   ☐ Industry

☐ Power generation   ☐ Land-use change and deforestation

> **TIP**
>
> Remember – when you are drawing a divided bar chart, make sure you order the categories from largest to smallest.

5 Delhi is a city in India with a population of more than 32 million.
It is ranked second in India for sulfur-dioxide emissions.
Figure 5.4 is a graph showing sulfur-dioxide concentration measured
in the air in Delhi from 2012 to 2021.

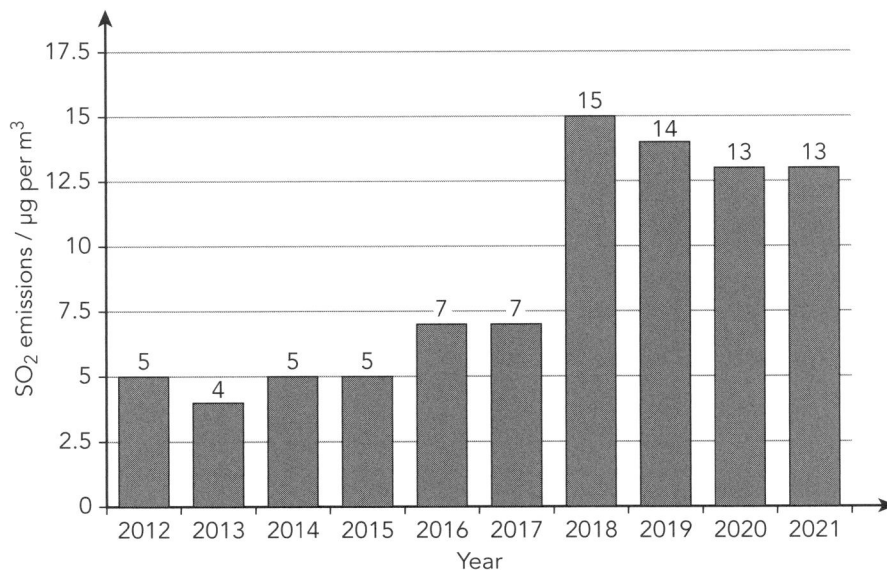

Figure 5.4: Concentrations of sulfur dioxide in the air in Delhi, India, 2012–2021.

a What is the mean concentration of SO_2 emissions / µg per m^3.

....

b What is the range of SO_2 emissions / µg per m^3? Show your workings.

....

6 A student decided to conduct their own research into sulfur-dioxide
concentrations in Delhi by testing the pH value of precipitation. They selected
three sample sites across the city – A, B and C. The most industrialised areas in
the city lie in the east. The student collected precipitation at 6 p.m. every Friday
for four weeks during the rainy season. They used a conical flask with a 1000 ml
volume, with a funnel covered in mesh. The equipment was kept 1 m above
ground. The student emptied the flask into a container and measured the
pH of the precipitation. The results are shown in Table 5.5.

Site	pH max	pH min	pH mean
A	5.4	4.2	5.1
B	6.0	4.9	5.2
C	7.5	5.8	6.8

Table 5.5: Results of research into sulfur-dioxide concentrations in Delhi.

a Suggest why the student chose the rainy season to collect the data.

....

....

b Suggest a reason why the funnel was covered in mesh.

....

c Suggest a reason why the equipment was kept 1 m above ground.

....

d Which sample site is most likely to be in the east of the city? Suggest a reason why.

Sample site: ....

Reason: ....

....

e Suggest how the student could improve their data collection.

....

....

....

> Ozone depletion
Exercise 5.4

LEARNING INTENTIONS

In this exercise you will:

- explain what the ozone hole is
- describe how ozone is depleted
- interpret a graph on ozone depletion
- identify the impacts of ozone depletion
- describe some strategies for managing ozone depletion
- show your understanding of key vocabulary on the topic of the atmosphere.

1 What do you understand by the term 'the ozone hole'?

....

....

2 Name the main group of gases that causes ozone depletion.

....

3 Describe how the release of these gases causes ozone depletion.

....

....

4 Figure 5.5 shows the maximum daily extent of the ozone depletion area between 1979 and 2021. Describe the trend shown by the graph.

....

....

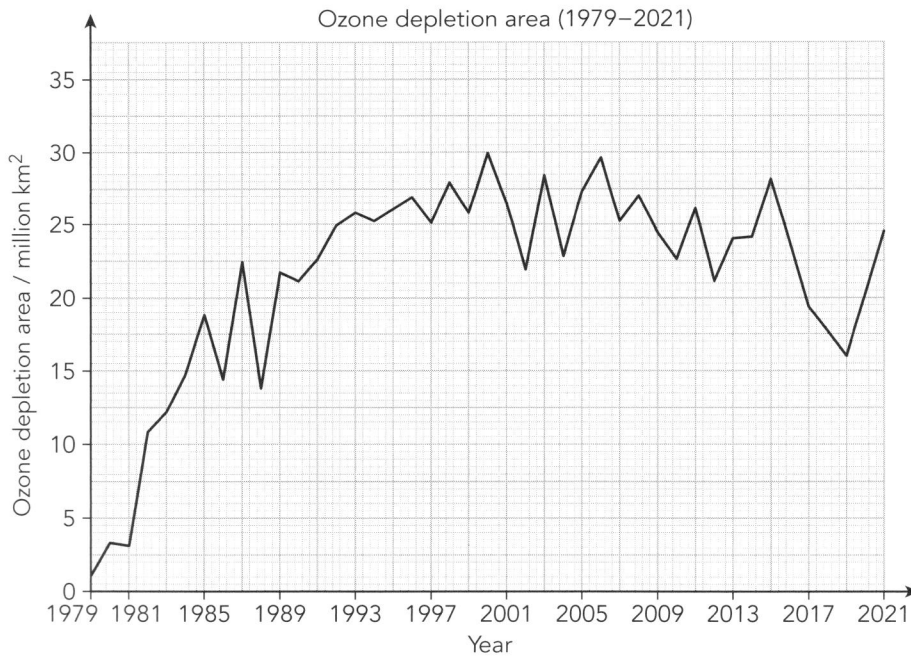

Figure 5.5: Maximum daily extent of the ozone depletion area, 1979–2021.

5 Describe the possible impacts of reduced stratospheric ozone for life on Earth.

....

....

....

6   Suggest **two** strategies that could be used to prevent ozone depletion.
Give one benefit and one limitation of each strategy.

a   ....

Benefit: ....

....

Limitation: ....

....

b   ....

Benefit: ....

....

Limitation: ....

....

7   Complete the word puzzle to show your understanding of the key vocabulary
relating to the atmosphere and human activities.

Across

6 Precipitation with a pH of 5.6 or less. (4, 4)

9 The main gas in the atmosphere. (8)

10 The lowest layer of the atmosphere. (11)

11 Ozone is concentrated in this atmosphere layer. (12)

12 A gas that contributes to acid rain. (6, 7)

13 Ultraviolet radiation is absorbed by this gas. (5)

14 Technology that helps to reduce acid rain. (9, 9)

Down

1 An example of a greenhouse gas. (7)

2 The number of layers in the atmosphere. (4)

3 Radiation emitted by the Sun. (5, 4)

4 The force that holds the atmosphere to Earth. (7)

5 Temperature does this with height in the lowest layer of the atmosphere. (8)

7 Gas used by plants in photosynthesis. (6, 7)

8 The upper limit of the mesosphere. (9)

14 The Montreal Protocol banned these gases. (4)

Chapter 6

Ecosystems, biodiversity and fieldwork

> Ecosystem interactions

Exercise 6.1

<table>
<tr>
<td>

LEARNING INTENTIONS

In this exercise you will:

- define key terms relating to ecosystems
- explain **biotic** and **abiotic** interactions
- explore the process of photosynthesis
- suggest how animals compete in an ecosystem
- compare different types of pollination
- describe the problems caused by invasive species.

</td>
<td>

KEY WORDS

biotic: living components of the environment that may affect other living things

abiotic: non-living components of the environment that may affect living things

</td>
</tr>
</table>

1   Write definitions of these terms:

ecosystem: ....

....

population: ....

....

community: ....

....

habitat: ....

....

niche: ....

....

2   Name **two** biotic and **two** abiotic factors in a woodland ecosystem.

....

....

....

....

3   Name the biotic interaction that is happening in each of the following pictures.

a   b   c

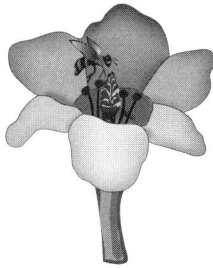      

a   ....

b   ....

c   ....

4   Explain in detail why a plant given water, carbon dioxide and a light source
     (all the requirements for the manufacture of glucose by the plant) would still not
     grow very well.

....

....

....

....

....

5   Briefly explain the role of chlorophyll in nature.

....

....

....

....

6   Complete the table to compare the features of flowers that are pollinated by wind and by insects.

Feature	Flowers pollinated by wind	Flowers pollinated by insects
Petals		
Anthers and stamens		
Stigma		
Pollen		
Scent		
Nectar		

> Energy flow in ecosystems

Exercise 6.2

LEARNING INTENTIONS

In this exercise you will:

- draw a **food web**

- interpret data and sketch **pyramids of numbers** and **pyramids of energy**

- show your understanding of the carbon cycle

- compare types of energy.

KEY WORD

food web:
a diagram showing the relationship between all (or most) of the producers, primary, secondary and tertiary consumers in an ecosystem

1   On a rocky beach, barnacles feed on phytoplankton. Dog whelks eat barnacles and mussels. The mussels also feed on phytoplankton. Mussels are commonly eaten by starfish. Dog whelks and starfish are eaten by birds, such as oystercatchers.

Draw a food web for the rocky beach, using the information in the passage above.

KEY WORDS

pyramid of numbers: a diagram that represents the numbers of organisms at each feeding (trophic) level in an ecosystem by a horizontal bar whose length is proportional to the numbers at that level

pyramid of energy: a diagram that represents the energy found at different trophic levels of an ecosystem

herbivore: another name for primary consumer

PEER ASSESSMENT

In pairs, compare your food webs from question 1. Discuss these questions.

• How do the food webs differ?

• How are they similar?

• Do you think they could be truly different? Why, or why not?

TIP

A food web will always have the producer at the beginning, and then the rest following on. Arrows always go from eaten to eater, and show the flow of energy.

2   In a survey of an area of rocky beach, the following figures were found:

Animal type	Numbers in fixed area
Barnacles	1 000 000
Dog whelks	100
Mussels	20
Oystercatchers	1
Starfish	3

Table 6.1: Numbers of animal types found in a fixed area of a rocky beach.

a   Sketch a pyramid of numbers for this part of the ecosystem.
On your sketch, show the actual numbers at each level.

b   The survey was unable to get figures for the primary producers for this
pyramid. Explain why this might have been the case.

....

....

....

....

TIP

Remember, a pyramid
of numbers will not
always be pyramid
shaped, or a triangle.
For example, if the
herbivore in an
ecosystem was a
sheep, it might have
hundreds of mites or
ticks feeding on it.

3   Complete the table using the information in it and the data from Table 6.1.
Then use the information from your completed table to draw a pyramid of
energy for this ecosystem.

Organism	Mass of one specimen (g)	Energy content (kJ per gram)	Total energy in the area (kJ)
Barnacle	0.05	6	
Mussel	10	7	
Dog whelk	5	5	
Starfish	500	8	
Oystercatcher	500	10	

4   Figure 6.1 is a diagram of the carbon cycle. Name substances A and C and
     processes B and D.

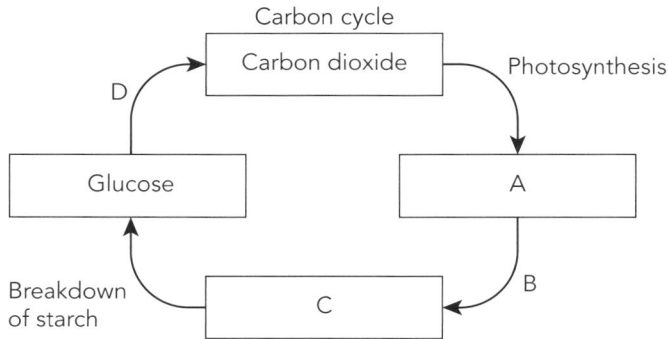

Figure 6.1: The carbon cycle.

A   ....

B   ....

C   ....

D   ....

5   Both photosynthesis and respiration involve energy. Explain the two processes in
     terms of energy.

     ....

     ....

     ....

> Forest ecosystems

Exercise 6.3

LEARNING INTENTIONS

In this exercise you will:

- analyse some data about deforestation

- interpret and explain changes to forest cover

- describe the role of deforestation in soil erosion

- show your understanding of carbon sinks and carbon stores

- explain the link between deforestation and global warming.

1   The rate of deforestation in the Amazon basin is estimated to be 0.52% of the entire area per year. This is equivalent to 18 857 km². Calculate the total area of the Amazon basin.

   ....

   ....

2   A major factor driving deforestation is the construction of roads. A study looked at the relationship between distance from a road and the extent of deforestation, and also the effect of protection. The data are shown on the graph in Figure 6.2.

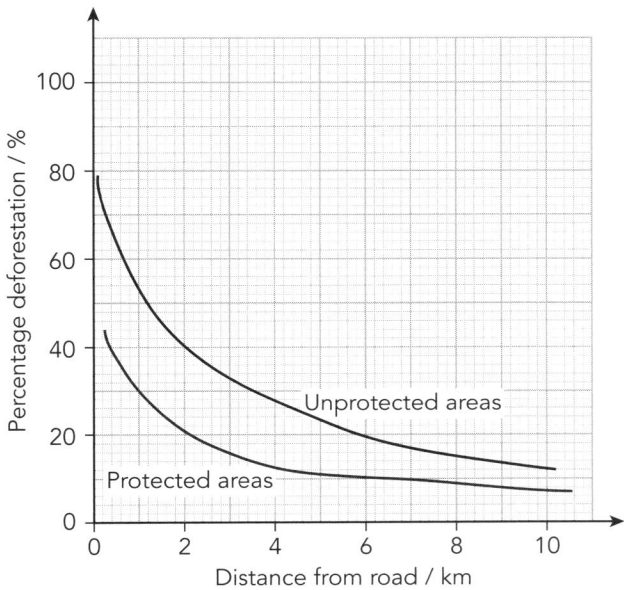

Figure 6.2: A graph showing the relationship between deforestation and distance from the road.

What is the percentage deforestation at 4 km from the road in a protected area and in an unprotected area?

   ....

   ....

3 Figure 6.3 shows two maps of an area in Madagascar, as it would have looked about 15 million years ago and as it looks today.

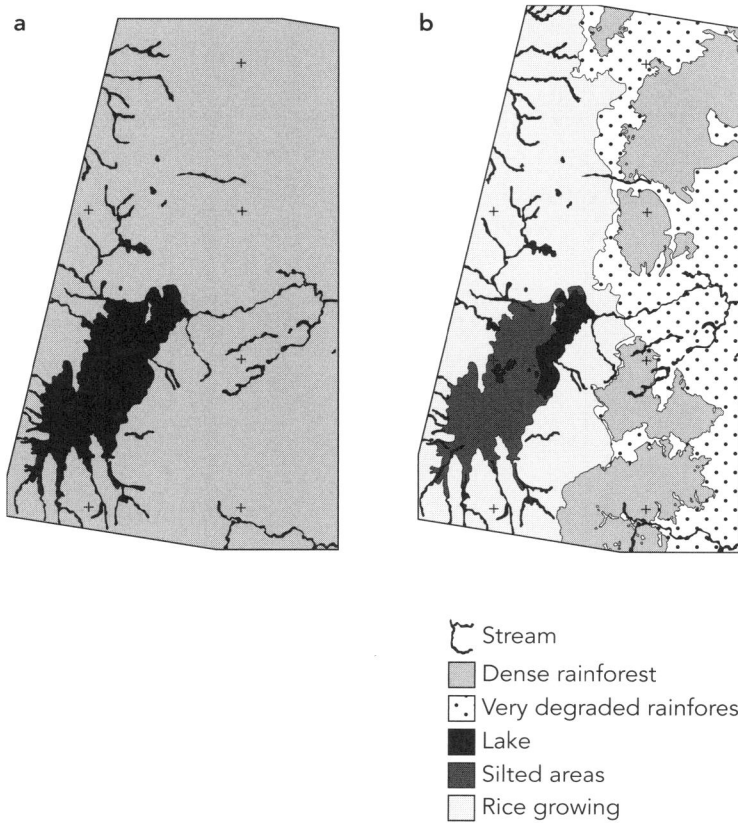

Stream
Dense rainforest
Very degraded rainforest
Lake
Silted areas
Rice growing

Figure 6.3: Two maps of the Lake Alaotra region in Madagascar showing **a** how it would have looked 15 million years ago and **b** how it looks today.

a Describe the changes in

  i the size and shape of the lake

  ....

  ....

  ....

  ii the extent of the rainforest

  ....

  ....

  ....

b   Suggest an explanation for the changes you have described in part a.
Use the following terms:

silting   deforestation   farming   cultivated rice   soil erosion

....

....

....

....

4   What is the difference between a carbon sink and a carbon store?

....

....

....

....

5   Describe how rainforests protect an area against soil erosion.

....

....

....

....

....

6   Explain why the cutting down of mature forest will not lead to a rise in
carbon dioxide levels – and therefore global warming – until the trees are burnt.

....

....

....

....

> Managing biodiversity

Exercise 6.4

LEARNING INTENTIONS

In this exercise you will:

- explain the meaning of 'sustainability'

- compare the productivity of mixed forestry and **monoculture**

- consider wildlife corridors as a strategy for **conservation**

- explore the use of seed banks

- analyse data and describe trends in graphs about tourism.

KEY WORDS

monoculture: the practice of growing only one crop or keeping only one type of animal on an area of farmland

conservation: the protection and management of natural areas

ecotourism: tourism in which the participants travel to see the natural world, ideally in a sustainable way

1   'One strategy for the conservation of biodiversity of an ecosystem is the sustainable harvesting of wild plants and animals.' Explain what 'sustainable' means in the context of this sentence.

   ....

   ....

   ....

   ....

   ....

2   Rubber is grown in either a mixed situation with other plants (called jungle rubber) or in a monoculture, with rubber trees only. Jungle rubber produces 590 kg/ha/year, whereas monoculture produces 1310 kg/ha/year. Calculate how many times more productive monoculture is than jungle rubber.

   ....

   ....

3 a Figure 6.4 shows some important wildlife areas that contain similar species. Mark the map to show how wildlife corridors could improve the conservation of these species.

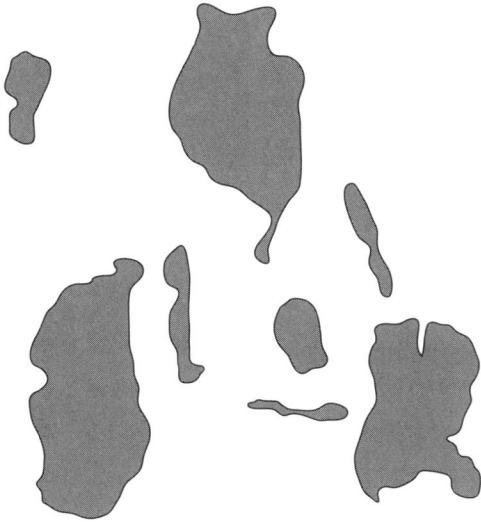

Figure 6.4: Fragmented wildlife areas.

b Give two limitations to the use of wildlife corridors as a conservation strategy.

i ....

....

ii ....

....

4 Zoos often maintain a studbook on animals they are breeding, which contains information about the parents, grand-parents etc. of the animals.. What use can zoos – and other organisations and individuals – make of such a studbook?

....

....

....

....

....

5 Explain why a government might decide to set up a seed bank rather than conserve living plants.

....

....

....

....

....

6 Table 6.2 shows a breakdown of the seed stored in global seed banks by type of crop.

Type of crop	% stored in seed bank
Cereals	53
Legumes	13
Vegetables	11
Grasses used for grazing livestock (forage)	7
Fruits and nuts	6
Industrial crops	6
Others	4

Table 6.2: Seed stores in global seed banks by crop type.

a Show this information in a pie chart.

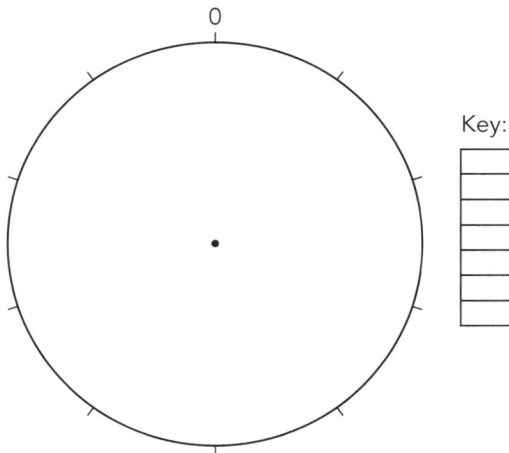

b Figure 6.5 shows a drawing of the global seed bank on the island of Spitsbergen in the Svalbard archipelago, north of Norway, in the Arctic Circle. Use your own knowledge and the information in the figure to suggest why this site and design is suitable.

....

....

....

....

....

....

....

....

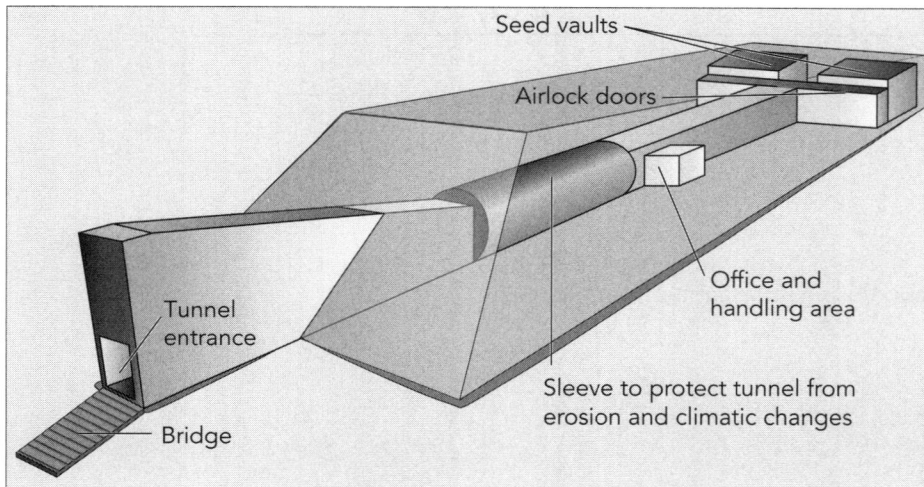

Figure 6.5: The global seed bank on Svalbard.

7 Whale watching is a form of **ecotourism**. Table 6.3 shows the top ten results of a report on the numbers of people who went on whale-watching trips by country.

Country	People
USA	4 899 809
Australia	1 635 374
Canada	1 165 684
Canary Islands	611 000
South Africa	567 367
New Zealand	546 445
China	307 000
Argentina	244 432
Brazil	228 946
Scotland	223 941
Total for top ten	10 429 998
Global total	**12 977 218**

Table 6.3: The top ten whale-watching countries.

a What percentage of global whale watching is carried out by the top ten countries?

....

b Complete the bar chart using information from the table.

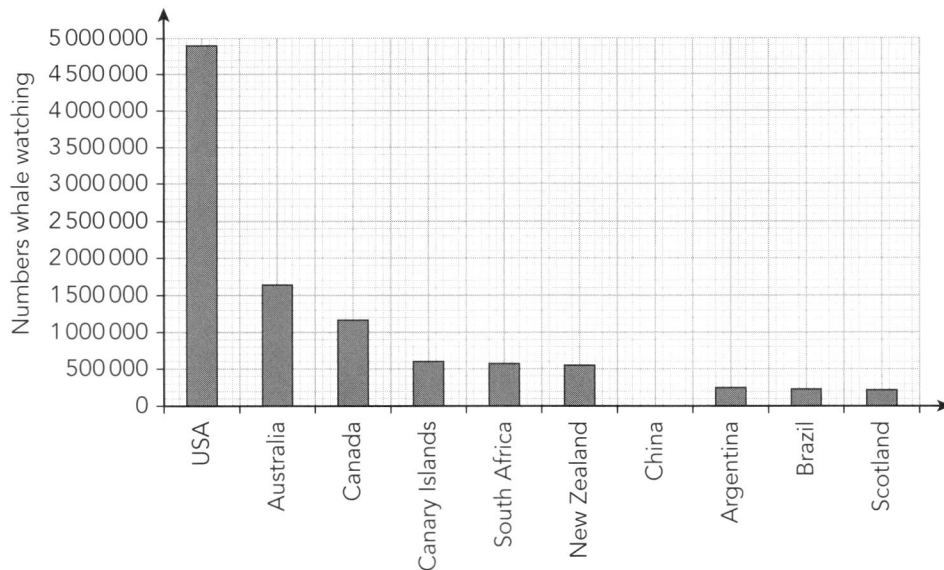

8   Figure 6.6 shows the growth in worldwide tourism over 17 years.

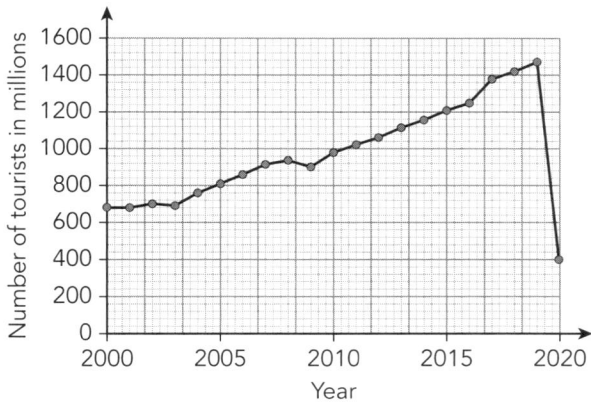

Figure 6.6: Worldwide growth in tourism, 2000–2020.

a   Describe the trends shown in the graph.

....

....

....

....

....

b   Suggest the likely environmental consequences of the trend you
    have described.

....

....

....

....

....

> **TIP**
>
> When describing
> a trend in a graph
> (or other resource)
> look for the general
> direction(s) shown.
> Do not discuss each
> minor 'wobble' in
> the data.

c   Suggest **three** ways in which any undesirable consequences of the changes in
    tourism over time might be reduced.

    i   ....

    ii ....

    iii ....

> Data collection through fieldwork investigation

Exercise 6.5

LEARNING INTENTIONS

In this exercise you will:

- plan an investigation

- show your understanding of sampling methods

- explore the benefits and limitations of a particular sampling technique

- use different sampling methods and sampling types

- estimate the size of natural populations

- carry out an investigation and evaluate the results.

KEY WORDS

transect: a sampling method in which sampling devices are laid out along a line already placed across an area

systematic sampling: a sampling method in which the sampling device is placed along a line or some other pre-determined pattern, the most common pattern being the line of a transect

random sampling: a sampling method in which the sampling device is placed using random number tables or a random number generator

1   Ants have made a trail through some grassland. Explain how you could investigate the effect the ants have had on the vegetation on the trail compared to that on either side of it. Use a diagram to help your explanation.

....

....

....

....

....

2   Match the sampling methods to the organisms. Write A, B or C in the boxes.

A Pooter and net   B Quadrat   C Pitfall trap

a   Barnacles stuck to rocks

b   Lichens on tree trunks

c   Ground beetles running around in a meadow

d   Mosquitoes

3   The following list shows some benefits and some limitations of camera trapping as a sampling method.

A   A large amount of data is generated.

B   It is not always clear whether animals seen in the camera trap are the same individual or different ones.

C   It is usually quite quick to set up a camera trap.

D   The camera needs to be in the right place, otherwise a lot of information may be missed.

E   Camera traps can be used in remote areas because they can be battery operated.

F   The batteries needed for a long life in cameras are expensive.

G   If bait is put out near the camera trap, animals may become 'trap happy', which means they will be over-sampled.

H   Thieves may target camera traps because they are valuable equipment.

I   Changes in the position of vegetation due to wind and rain can obscure the view of the camera trap after setting up.

J   Artificial intelligence can be used to sort through camera trap images and discard false positives and negatives.

a   Write the letter for each statement in the correct column of the table.
    Some statements might fit in both columns.

b   In the table, add one more benefit and one more limitation.

Benefits	Limitations

4   Figure 6.7 shows a meadow surrounded by trees. Explain how you could sample
    the plants in the meadow.

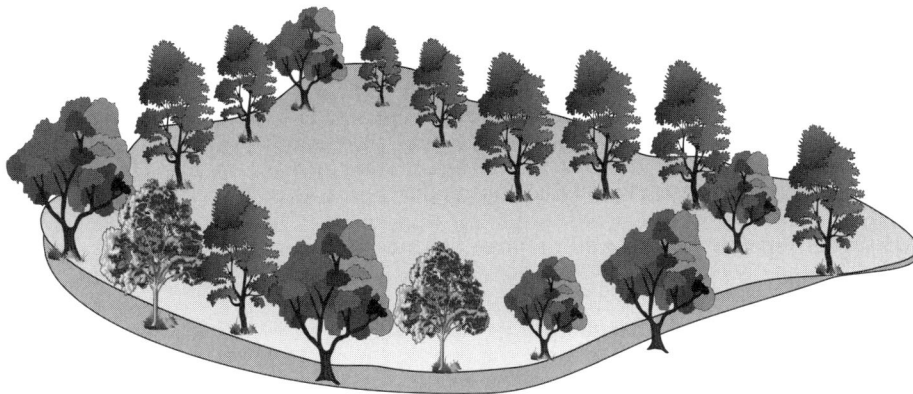

Figure 6.7: A possible sampling area.

....

....

....

....

....

....

....

....

5   Firebreaks are cut through forests to avoid the spread of fire from one section to another. However, removal of valuable forest habitat is a concern.

Figure 6.8 shows a section through a primary forest at the place where a firebreak has been cut.

Figure 6.8: A firebreak through a section of primary forest.

An ecologist carried out a survey using standard techniques to assess the impact of firebreak cutting on biodiversity in the forest shown. Figure 6.9 shows an aerial view of the firebreak and the surrounding forest.

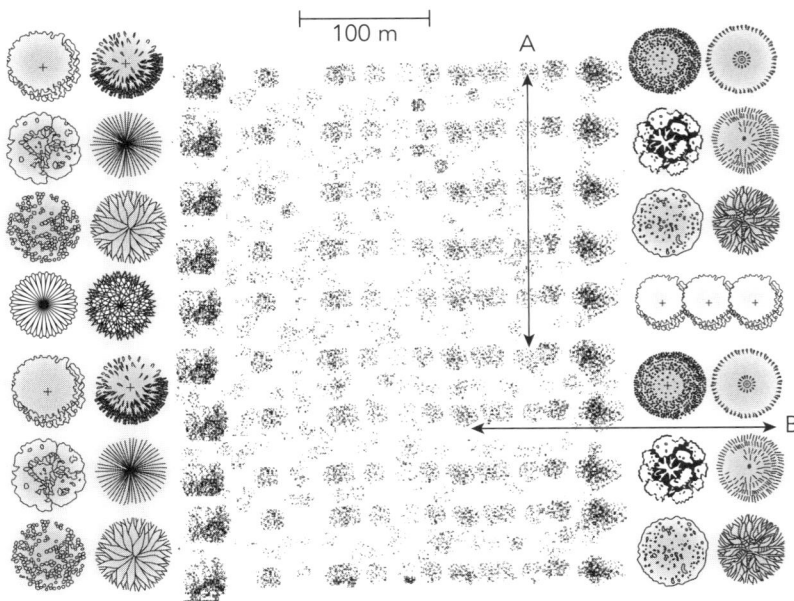

Figure 6.9: An aerial view of the firebreak through the forest.

a   The ecologist considered two possible **transect** positions to assess the effect, A and B. Explain why the ecologist chose position B.

....

....

....

....

b Calculate how many quadrats would be required to place one every 20 metres along the transect line in position B.

....

....

....

....

c Figure 6.10 shows a quadrat placed at 80 metres from the start. There are four species of plants, A,B,C and D, within it.

Figure 6.10: A quadrat placed 80 metres from the start.

Estimate the cover of each plant species shown using the ACFOR scale. On this scale the following apply:

A = abundant

C = common

F = frequent

O = occasional

R = rare

....

....

....

....

d   Use the quadrat in Figure 6.10 to estimate percentage cover of plants A,B,C and D using any method you choose. Explain the method you have used and how you have applied it to this quadrat.

....

....

....

....

....

....

e   Draw a table in which the results of the first five quadrats of position B could be recorded, assuming eight species were found (it would almost certainly be more than this).

f   Both position B and position A use **systematic sampling**. Another ecologist suggested that the question about the effect of the firebreak on the biodiversity of the forest could be investigated using a **random sampling** technique. Suggest how a random sampling method could be used to help to answer this question.

....

....

....

....

....

....

6 Common duckweed is a pest in lakes and rivers. It divides frequently, so the plant quickly covers any body of water into which it has been introduced. However, one benefit of duckweed in a water body is that it may remove toxic chemicals.

In an investigation, the effect of the toxic chemical on duckweed growth was studied as follows.

- Six containers were labelled A to F

- Each container was filled with the same volume of water with different concentrations of toxic chemicals in each

- The pH of each container was 7.0

- Duckweed plants were collected from an unpolluted lake

- Ten plants were placed in each container

- The containers were placed in a room held at 20°C and with a set of lights over them

- The number of plants in each pot was recorded after two weeks.

a State the independent and dependent variables in this investigation.

Independent variable: ....

....

Dependent variable: ....

....

b Suggest a suitable hypothesis for this investigation.

....

....

....

c What was the aim of this investigation?

....

....

d List **two** control variables in this investigation.

i ....

ii ....

e Suggest how the investigation could be modified to allow for the identification of anomalies in the results.

....

....

....

....

7 The results of the investigation were as follows.

• In each of containers, A to F, the number of plants at the start was 10.

• After 14 days, the number of plants in container A was 18, B 21, C 25, D 15, E 13 and F 11.

• The concentration of toxic chemicals (in ppm) in A was 0.0, in B 0.5, in C 0.75, in D 1.0, in E 2.0 and in F. 5.0.

a Make a table to show all of these results, and to show the change in the number of plants from day 1 to day 14.

b What conclusion can you make from these results?

....

....

....

....

PEER ASSESSMENT

In small groups, discuss how you answered question 5d. Did you all do it the same way? If not, which ways do you think were the best and why? If other members of the group did it in the same way as you, see if you can find someone who did it differently and discuss the differences with them.

> Chapter 7
Natural hazards

> Tectonic activity

Exercise 7.1

LEARNING INTENTIONS
In this exercise you will:
• identify the world's continents and oceans
• define key terminology relating to tectonic activity
• draw diagrams of different plate boundaries.

KEY WORD
mantle: the mantle is found between the crust and core and is the thickest section of the Earth.

1   Write the names of the seven continents and the five major oceans in the correct place on the map.

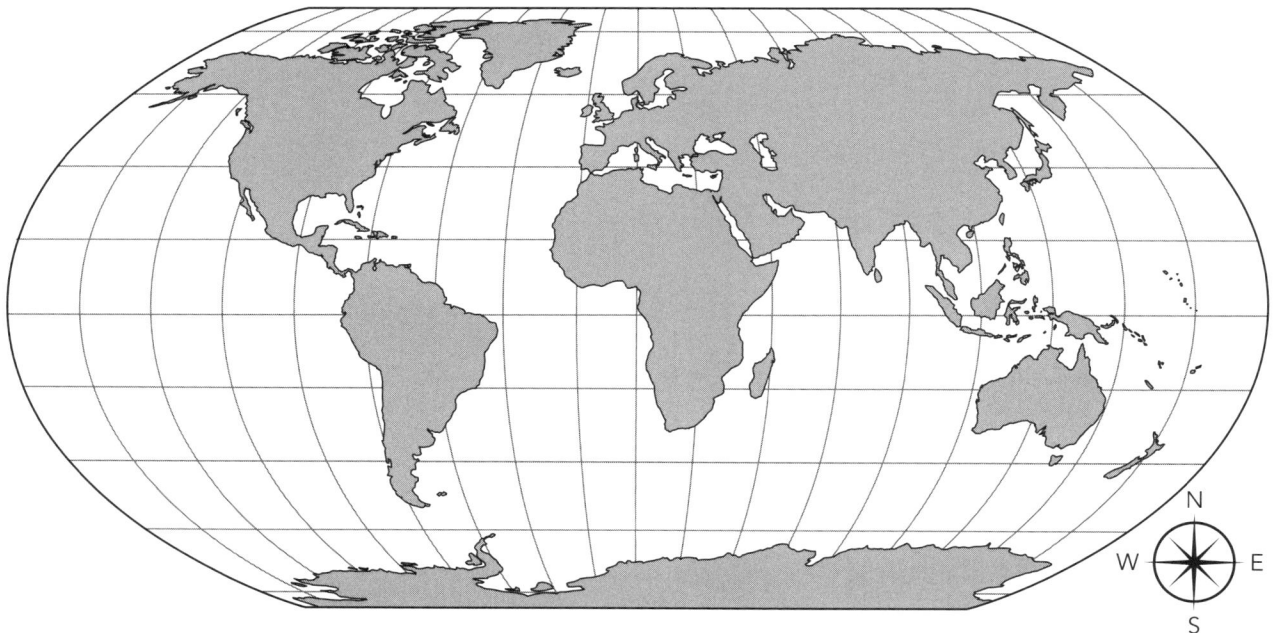

2 Choose the correct word from the list to complete each definition.

oceanic   destructive   lithosphere   fold mountains   oceanic trench

a Tectonic plate: a piece of .... that moves slowly on the **mantle**.

b Plate boundary: the place where two or more plates meet. There are three main types of plate boundary: constructive, ... and conservative.

c .... are created where two or more tectonic plates are pushed together. Rocks are compressed and folded upwards.

d Subduction zone: a zone where the .... plate is deflected down into the mantle. At the surface, the subduction zone coincides with ocean trenches.

e ....: a depression of the ocean floor which runs parallel to a destructive plate boundary.

3 In the space below, draw an annotated diagram to show the cross-section through a divergent (constructive) plate boundary. Label the following features on your diagram and give it a title.

North American Plate (oceanic)   Eurasian Plate (oceanic)

direction of plate movement   convection current   mid-ocean ridge

volcano   ocean   mantle

4   In the space below, draw an annotated diagram to show the cross-section through a convergent (destructive) plate boundary. Label the following features on your diagram and give it a title.

Nazca Plate (oceanic plate)   **South American Plate (continental plate)**

direction of plate movement   **mantle**   **ocean trench**   **subduction zone**

rising magma   **volcano**   **fold mountains (Andes)**

> Earthquakes and volcanic eruptions
Exercise 7.2

LEARNING INTENTIONS

In this exercise you will:

- show understanding of key terms relating to earthquakes
- identify features of a volcanic eruption
- present and interpret data about the impact of volcanic eruptions
- identify strategies to limit the impact of tectonic hazards
- explain why people live near volcanoes.

1   What is the difference between the focus and the epicentre of an earthquake?

....

....

KEY WORDS

pyroclastic flows: very hot gases, ash and fragmented rocks, which can reach speeds of over $100\,km\,h^{-1}$ at temperatures of 200 to $700\,°C$

tsunami: a large, fast-moving wave created by ocean floor displacement or landslides

2 Figure 7.1 shows the features of a volcanic eruption. Complete labels A, B, C and D to identify the missing features.

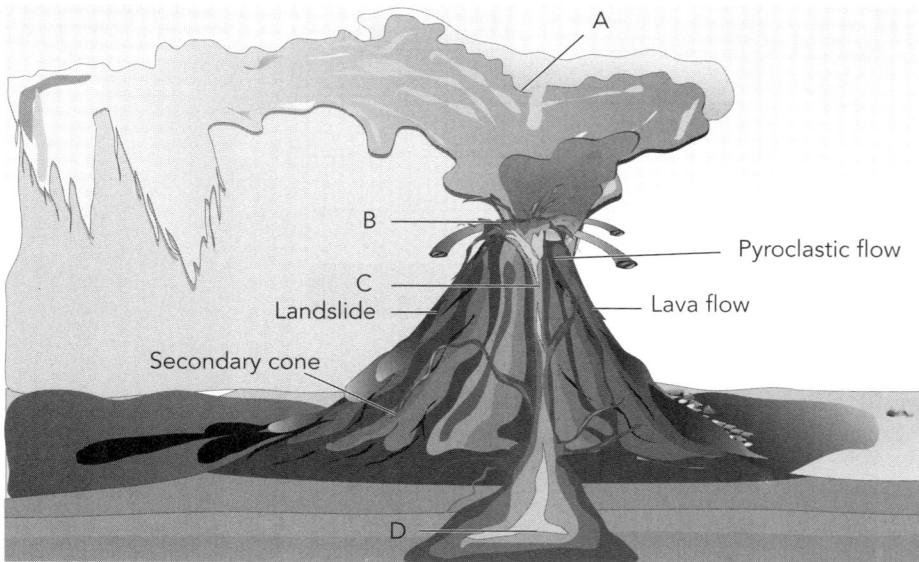

Figure 7.1: Features of a volcano.

A   ....

B   ....

C   ....

D   ....

3 Table 7.1 shows the estimated percentage of deaths by volcanic activity between 1920 and 2020 by region.

Region	% of deaths caused by volcanic activity, 1920–2020
Africa	5
North America	1
South and Central America	58
Asia	29
Europe	0.5
Oceania	6.5

Table 7.1: Estimated percentage of deaths due to volcanic activity, 1920–2020.

a   Use the data in the table and the key to draw a pie chart to display the data.

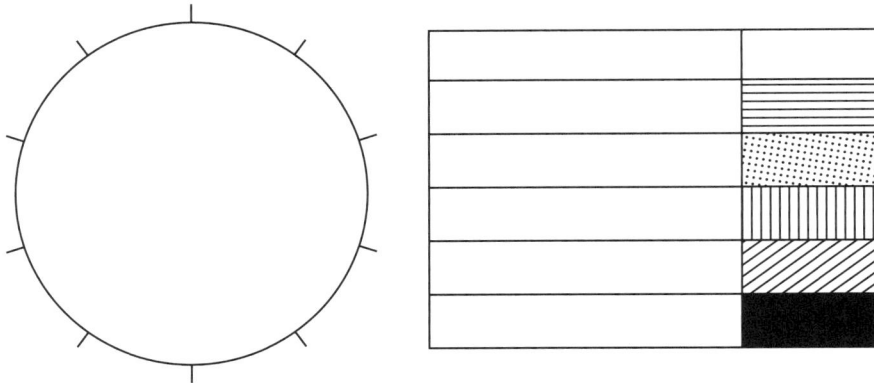

b   In which region of the world did most deaths from volcanic activity occur between 1920 and 2020? Suggest **three** reasons why this was the case.

Region: ....

Reason 1: ....

....

Reason 2: ....

....

Reason 3: ....

....

4   Table 7.2 shows the primary causes of death by the ten volcanoes that killed most people between 1930 and 2018.

Volcano	Country	Year	Deaths by pyroclastic flow	Deaths by landslides	Deaths by ashfall	Deaths by gas	Deaths by tsunami
Merapi	Indonesia	1930	1 369				
Tavurvur	Papua New Guinea	1937	507				
Lamington	Papua New Guinea	1951	2 942				
Hibok-Hibok	Philippines	1951	500				
Agung	Indonesia	1963	1 148				
El Chichon	Mexico	1982	2 000				
Nevado del Ruiz	Colombia	1985		23 000			
Lake Nyos	Cameroon	1986				1 700	
Pinatubo	Philippines	1991			300		
Anak Krakatoa	Indonesia	2018					437

Table 7.2: Primary causes of death from volcanic activity, 1930–2018.

Present the data in rank order of cause of death, from the highest to lowest.

Primary cause of death	Number of deaths

5 Complete the spider diagram to show four different strategies that can be used to prevent loss of life from a tectonic hazard.

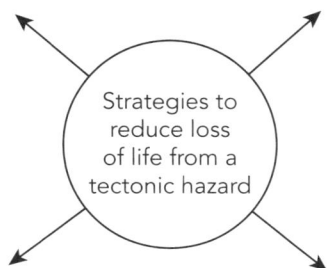

Strategies to reduce loss of life from a tectonic hazard

6 Explain why people are still prepared to live near volcanoes.

....

....

....

....

....

....

....

....

> Tropical cyclones

Exercise 7.3

1   Complete the passage using words from the list.

hurricanes	87	5° to 30°	clockwise	13	low	27
anticlockwise	119	high	eye	0° to 15°	typhoons	

Tropical cyclones are ....-pressure weather systems that produce

winds of .... km per hour or greater. They develop in the tropics

between latitudes .... north or south of the equator, where the

surface ocean temperatures are greater than .... °C.

The ocean depth needs to be at least 60m.

In the northern hemisphere, winds rotate around an area of calm called the

.... in an .... direction. Tropical cyclones are

called .... if they form over the north-west Pacific Ocean.

2 Table 7.3 shows the number of typhoons recorded in each month of the year from 1960 to 2023 in the western Pacific.

Month	Number of typhoons
January	28
February	14
March	26
April	37
May	76
June	116
July	261
August	394
September	350
October	269
November	139
December	69

Table 7.3: Typhoons recorded per month, 1960–2023.

a The month with the lowest number of recorded typhoons was ....

b The month with the highest number of recorded typhoons was ....

c State the percentage of typhoons that were recorded in the month with the highest number.

....

d Using information in Table 7.3, state which months of the year are typhoon season.

....

....

3 Figure 7.2 shows some advice given to people by the authorities in western Pacific countries on how to manage impacts before and during a typhoon.

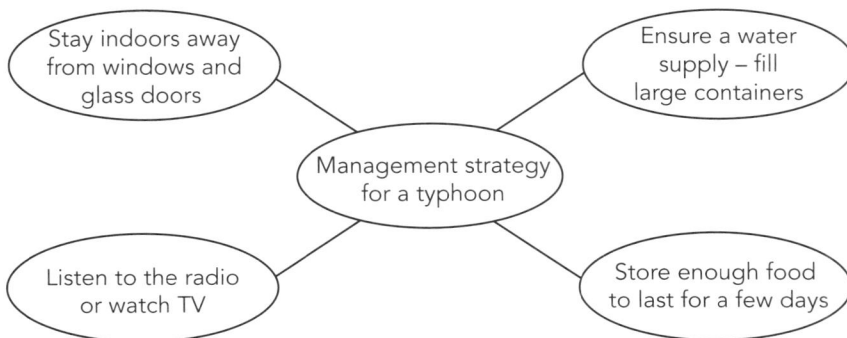

Figure 7.2: Strategies for dealing with typhoons.

Explain why people were given each of these pieces of advice.

....

....

....

....

....

....

....

....

PEER ASSESSMENT

Compare your answers with a partner. Did you come up with the same reasons for each of the pieces of advice? Add to or correct your answers to this question. What other strategies for managing the impacts of tropical cyclones can you think of? Write some additional suggestions here, then compare your ideas.

....

....

....

....

⟩ Flooding

Exercise 7.4

LEARNING INTENTIONS

In this exercise you will:

- define river flooding

- suggest a positive impact of flooding

- identify the causes of river flooding

- compare the impact of flooding in low-income countries (LICs) and middle-income countries (MICs)

- evaluate a strategy for managing floods.

KEY WORDS

infiltration: the process by which water seeps into the ground

impermeable: describing rock that water (or other liquids or gases) cannot pass through

1   What is meant by 'river flooding'?

....

....

....

....

2   State **one** positive impact of flooding.

....

....

3   There are many reasons why a river floods. Draw a line to link each cause of flooding to the correct explanation.

Cause of flooding
deforestation
previous weather
rock type
relief
heavy rainfall
urbanisation

Explanation
The **infiltration** capacity is quickly exceeded and overland flow takes place.
Concrete and tarmac are **impermeable** and lead to more overland flow.
If trees are removed there is less **interception** and infiltration.
Impermeable rock leads to greater overland flow.
The more saturated the soil, the less infiltration can take place.
Steeper gradients lead to faster overland flow.

4   Read the following passages about two flood events in 2022. The first flood occurred in Queensland, Australia (a high-income country (HIC)); the second was in Pakistan (an LIC).

Torrential rain has sent floodwaters to record levels in Australia

The Brisbane River, which flows through the state capital, Brisbane, has burst its banks. It has been reported that in just three days, Brisbane and southern Queensland received 80% of the annual amount of rainfall. Cars were washed into the sea and buildings were knee-deep in muddy water. Around 23 000 homes and businesses have been damaged. Thousands of people have been evacuated and 13 have lost their lives. Those affected will be able to claim damages and financial support from the Australian government.

Unprecedented floods hit Pakistan

Flooding has killed more than 1000 people and affected 33 million people. Around 1.1 million livestock have been swept away, and 75 000 km of agricultural land has been damaged. This is devastating, as most of the farmers in the Indus Valley survive by subsistence farming. Such a huge loss of agricultural land will lead to food insecurity. Relief organisations are worried that waterborne diseases such as dengue fever, cholera and malaria will break out in the overcrowded evacuation camps. Heavy rains have been blamed, with southern Pakistan receiving 350% more than average rainfall for the months of July and August. Glacier melting has increased river levels, but experts also say that deforestation has been taking place at a rapid pace.

a What was the common cause of flooding in these two events?

....

....

b How might deforestation in Pakistan contribute to the flooding?

....

....

....

....

c Compare the number of people who died in these two flooding events.

....

....

d Describe how the effects of the flooding in an HIC such as Australia are different from the effects in an LIC such as Pakistan.

....

....

....

....

....

....

How easy did you find it to extract the relevant information from the text?
Did you have to read the text more than once to get the answers?
Rate your confidence in this skill on a scale of 1 (very confident) to 5
(not confident at all). How could you improve at this type of task?

5   Hard engineering structures, such as levees, flood barriers, channels and dams, are
one strategy employed to reduce floods. Do you think they are suitable for use in
an LIC? Explain your answer.

....

....

....

....

....

....

....

....

> Drought

Exercise 7.5

LEARNING INTENTIONS

In this exercise you will:

- apply your knowledge of droughts

- practise drawing and analysing a climate graph

- develop an understanding of the impacts of droughts

- outline strategies to deal with droughts.

KEY WORD

malnutrition: not
having enough of the
correct nutrients to
eat, causing ill health

1   Each of the following four statements contains an error.
Rewrite the statements correctly.

a   Drought is when there is rain over a long period of time.

....

b Droughts only occur in Africa and South America.

....

c Drought is associated with low-pressure systems.

....

2 Figure 7.3 shows the location of Ethiopia, a country in East Africa.

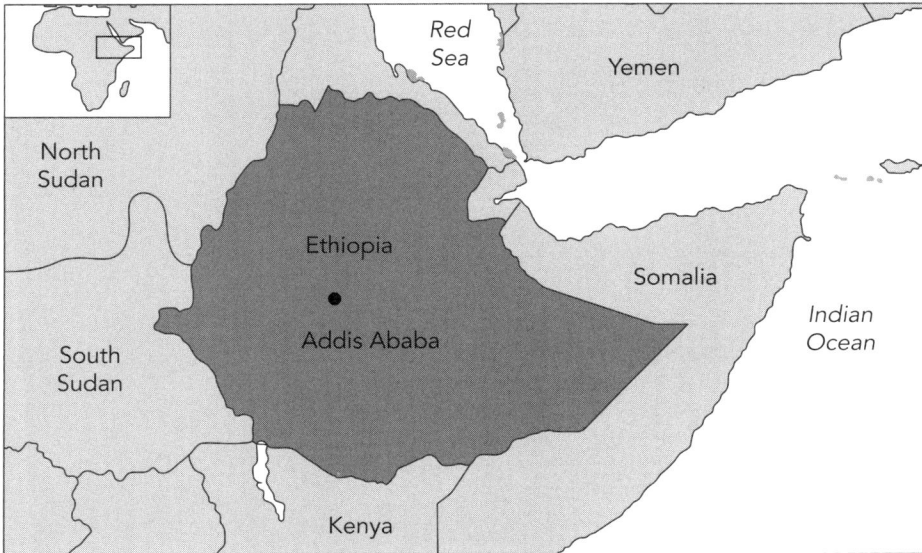

Figure 7.3: A map showing the location of Ethiopia.

> **TIP**
>
> A climate graph is a combined graph – that is, two types of graph containing related information presented on one chart. As temperature is continuous data, it is presented as a line graph. Rainfall is non-continuous data, so it requires a bar chart

a On the graph paper below, plot the mean monthly temperatures using a line graph, and the mean monthly rainfall using a bar chart, for Addis Ababa, the capital city of Ethiopia. Remember to label the axes.

	J	F	M	A	M	J	J	A	S	O	N	D
Mean monthly temperature (°C)	16	16	17	17	18	17	15	15	16	15	15	15
Mean monthly precipitation (mm)	20	32	54	56	96	112	245	270	117	40	10	13

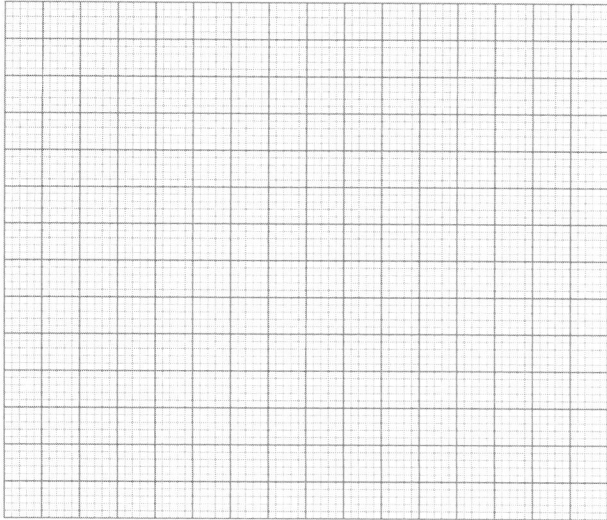

b What is the total mean annual rainfall? Circle **one** answer.

1006 mm   1065 mm   165 mm   1650 mm

c What is the annual range of temperature for Addis Ababa?

....

d Look again at the climate graph of Addis Ababa you have drawn.
In which months of the year do you think farmers will experience difficulties
in growing crops and raising livestock? Explain your answer.

....

....

....

....

3 Read the two passages below about the causes and effects of drought in two
contrasting areas of the world. Passage A is about Ethiopia and Passage B is
about China.

Passage A

In 2023, Ethiopia faced its sixth consecutive year of failed spring rains,
compounded by atmospheric conditions that reduced the summer rains. Farmers
did not have time to recover from the 2017 drought and subsequent locust
infestation. Charity organisations claimed that 12 million people were suffering
from food insecurity and would need emergency assistance if acute **malnutrition**
and fatalities were to be avoided. There were severe crop and livestock losses.
Farmers began selling off remaining livestock as they could no longer feed them,
and many farming families moved to urban areas.

Passage B

In 2022, the Yangtze River drainage basin faced its worst drought since 1961. Rainfall levels were 50% lower than in 2021, and average temperatures were 0.9°C higher than the same period the year before. Farming in this region of China depends on irrigation, but lakes and reservoirs dried up. Two-thirds of China's rice crop is grown along the Yangtze River, and there was concern over disrupted food supply. Output from hydro-electric power plants had to be reduced, causing factory closures, and homes and businesses had water restrictions. Estimated financial losses from the drought were put at US$7.6 billion.

a   Compare and contrast the causes of drought in Ethiopia and China.

   ....

   ....

   ....

   ....

   ....

   ....

b   How do the two extracts show that it is often countries at the lowest level of economic development that suffer most from natural hazards?

   ....

   ....

   ....

   ....

4   Suggest **two** sustainable methods of reducing the impact of droughts and explain how they work.

   Method 1: ....

   ....

   ....

   Method 2: ....

   ....

   ....

> Chapter 8

Human population

> Population density and distribution

Exercise 8.1

LEARNING INTENTIONS

In this exercise you will:

- define some key terms relating to human **populations**

- describe the distribution of the world population

- calculate population densities

- analyse data about population density

- identify countries as LICs, MICs or HICs.

KEY WORDS

population: all the organisms of one species living in a defined area

income: money received over a stated time period

1 Write brief definitions of the following terms.

Population density: ....

Population distribution: ....

Sparsely populated: ....

Densely populated: ....

2 Look at Figure 8.1. Write a description of the distribution of the human population.

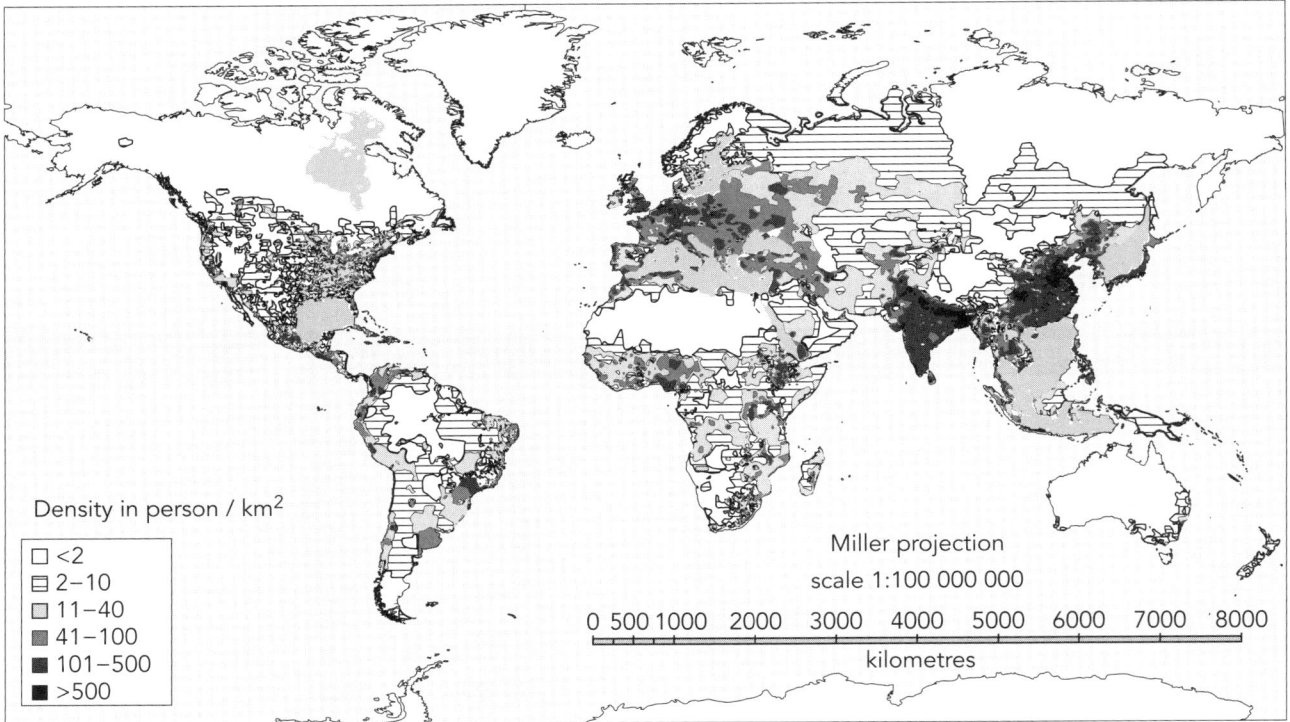

Figure 8.1: A world map showing global population distribution.

....

....

....

....

....

....

....

....

3 **a** In 2024, the population of Brazil was 217 431 446. The area of Brazil is 8.52 million km². Calculate the density of the Brazilian population in 2024.

....

....

b   In 2024, Bangladesh had a population of 174 406 748. The area of Bangladesh is 147 570 km². Calculate how many times denser the population of Bangladesh is compared than that of Brazil.

....

....

....

....

4   Table 8.1 shows information about the population and areas of the seven provinces of Costa Rica from the 2011 census. Calculate the population density of these seven provinces and add this data to the last column of the table. State which is the highest and which the lowest.

Province	Area (km²)	Population	Density (people per km²)
Heredia	2 657	433 677	
Cartago	3 124	490 903	
San José	4 966	1 404 242	
Limón	9 189	386 862	
Alajuela	9 757	885 571	
Guanacaste	10 141	354 154	
Puntarenas	11 266	410 929	

Table 8.1: Area and population of the seven provinces of Costa Rica.

Highest: ....

Lowest: ....

5   Figure 8.2 is a bar chart showing the percentage of the population that is rural for the seven most rural countries in the world. Why might Liechtenstein be considered a surprising inclusion in this list? Use Figure 8.3 to help you explain.

....

....

....

....

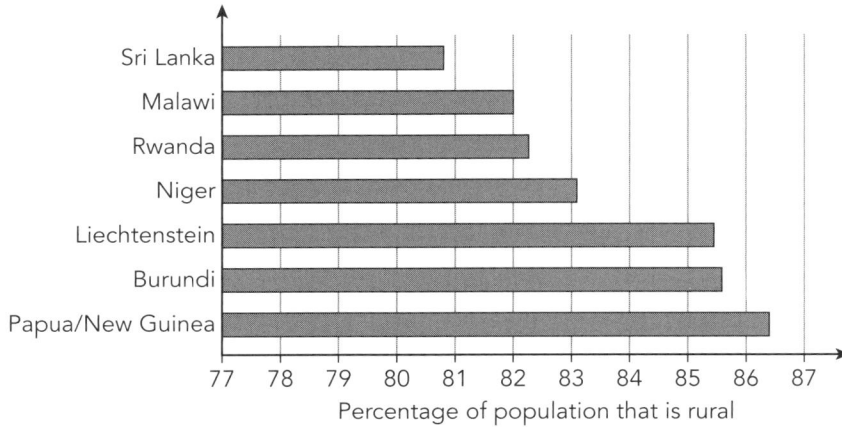

Figure 8.2: A bar chart showing the percentage of the population that lives in rural areas for the seven most rural countries.

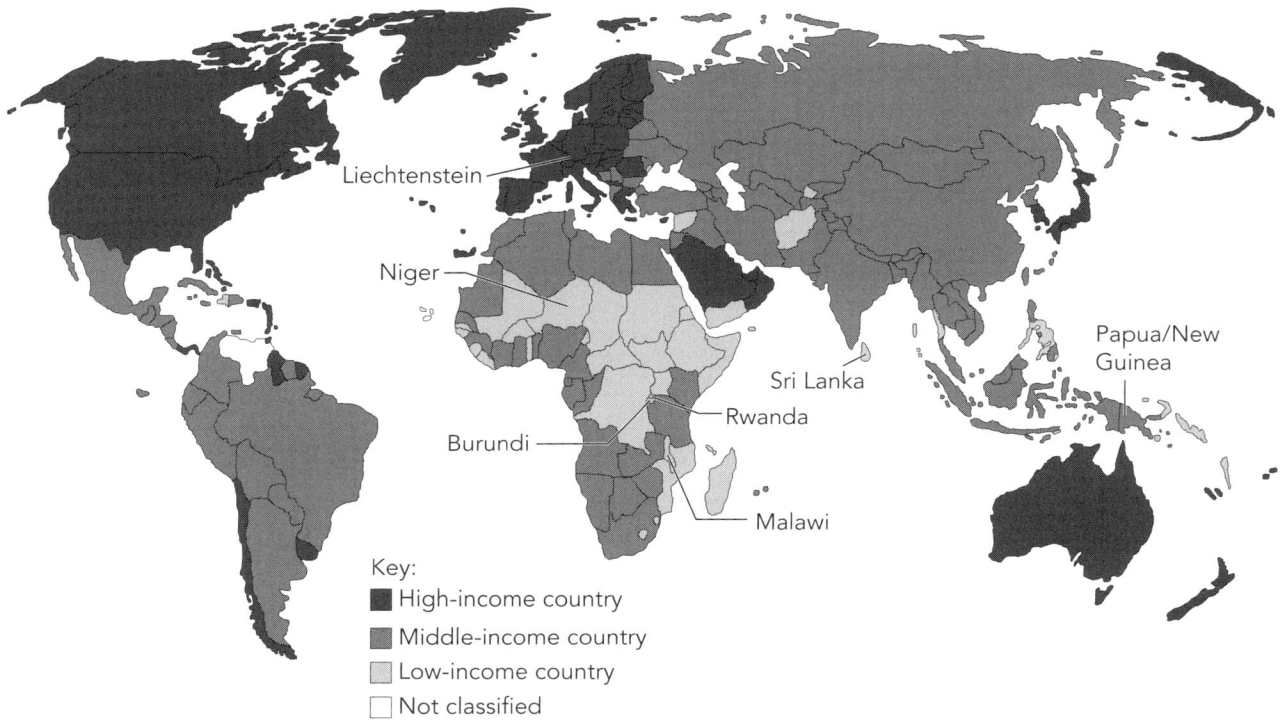

Figure 8.3: A map showing the distribution of high-, middle- and low-income countries around the world.

6 The table shows the gross national **income** (GNI) per capita of 10 countries or regions. Complete the table to rank the countries/regions in the list out of 10. Then decide if each one is an LIC, MIC or HIC.

Rank	Country or region	GNI per capita ($)	LIC, MIC or HIC
	French Polynesia (France)	18 560	
	New Caledonia (France)	13 210	
	Greenland (Denmark)	34 800	
	Liechtenstein	116 600	
	South Sudan	1 050	
	Yemen	840	
	Andorra	46 530	
	Cuba	8 920	
	Turkmenistan	7 080	
	Syria	760	

> Population structure

Exercise 8.2

LEARNING INTENTIONS

In this exercise you will:

- define 'structure' in the context of populations
- draw **population pyramids** to show declining and growing populations
- show understanding of dependent and independent populations
- compare the structures of different populations
- interpret a population pyramid.

KEY WORD

population pyramid: a diagram that shows the proportion of the population that is male and female in different age groups (usually five-year intervals)

1 What **two** factors are considered when we talk about the 'structure' of a population?

....

2   Sketch a population pyramid for a country in which the population is:

a   Growing

b   Declining

3   Tick the boxes to identify whether each person would be classed as a dependent or independent population.

		Dependent	Independent
a	A school-aged child	☐	☐
b	A young person studying at university	☐	☐
c	A young person working in their first job	☐	☐
d	A middle-aged person in a professional career	☐	☐
e	An elderly person who has retired	☐	☐

4   Compare the structure of the population pyramids for the two countries in Figure 8.4.

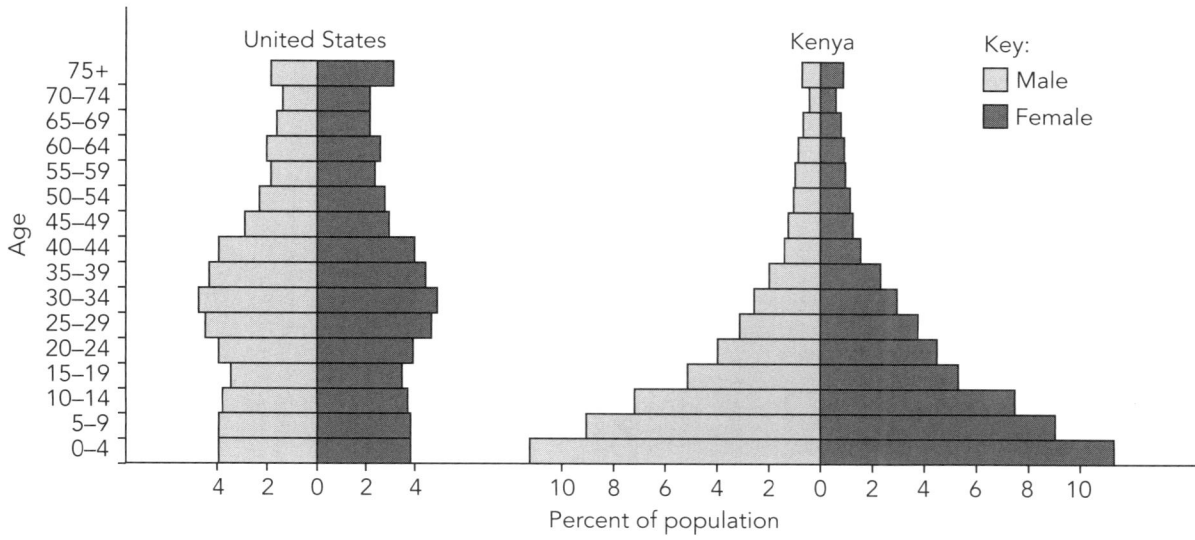

Figure 8.4: Population pyramids for the USA and Kenya.

....

....

....

....

....

....

5   Look at Figure 8.5.

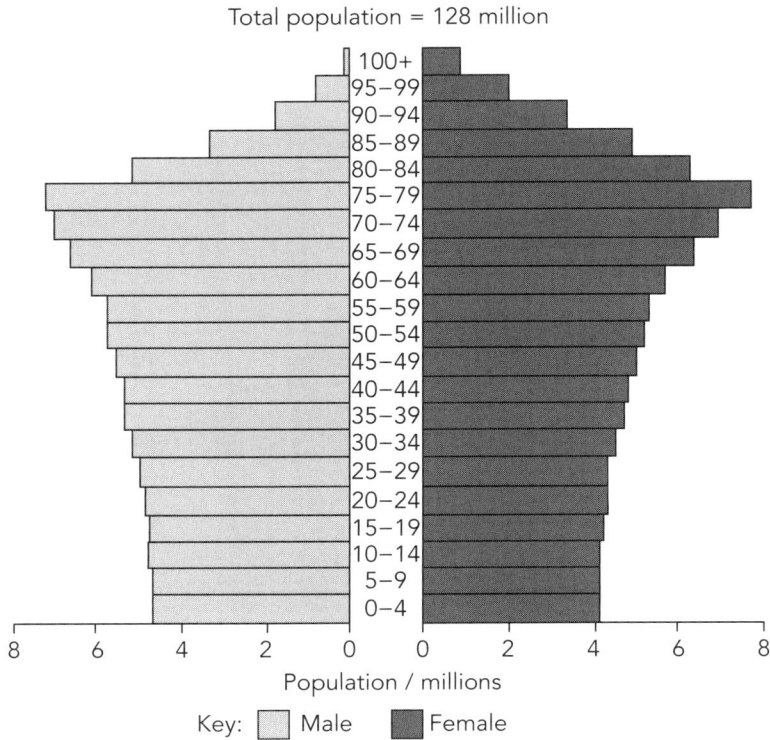

Figure 8.5: Population pyramid.

a   Determine the population of males who are aged 14 and under.

....

b   Calculate the percentage of the population who are female aged between 80 and 84.

....

> Population growth
Exercise 8.3

1   Draw lines to match the key terms with the correct definitions

Term
birth rate
death rate
rate of natural increase
life expectancy

Definition
The length of time that a living thing, especially a human being, is likely to live.
The total number of deaths over time.
The birth rate minus the death rate.
The total number of live births over time.

2   a   Complete the passage by putting the correct numbers in the gaps.

A pair of animals, male and female, is introduced into an area.

They produce four young, two males and two females. The parents die after

one year. The population will now number .... If these four

young produce four young for each pair, and then die, the population will be

.... after two years. If the pattern repeats itself, the population

will be .... after five years, 512 after .... years

and .... after 10 years.

b Plot the population numbers for years 1–10 on the graph.

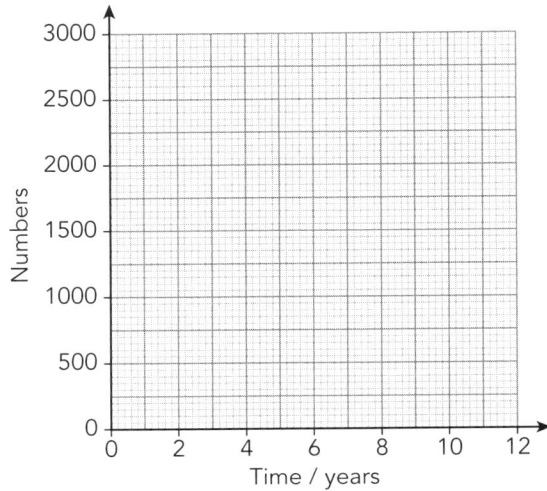

c What is this type of population growth called?

....

d In a different colour on your graph, show what would happen when the population reached the highest the environment can support – 3000.

3 Figure 8.6 shows estimated past human population (1800–1948), actual population records (1949–2020) and three possible predictions until 2100.

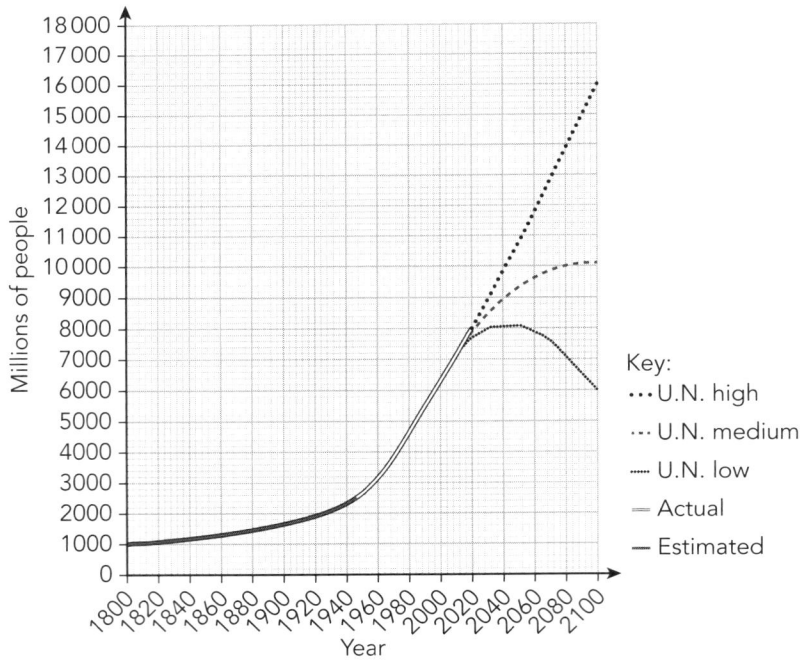

Figure 8.6: A graph showing estimated past population, actual population and population predictions to 2100.

a For how many years had the size of the human population been recorded up to 2020?

....

b What was the estimated population in 1800?

....

c i At what date was the human population 2 billion, and at what date was it at 4 billion?

....

ii Approximately how long did the population take to double in size from 2 billion?

....

....

d What will be the doubling time, if any, from 2020 in the case of each of the predictions?

Low: ....

Medium: ....

High: ....

e Give **two** reasons for the change between 1800 and 2000.

....

....

....

....

4 Complete the table.

Population	Birth rate per year	Death rate per year	Increase/decrease per year	Increase/decrease percentage
1 000 000	10 000	5 000	Increase by 5 000 per year	Increase by 0.5%
10 000 000	50 000	30 000		
5 000 000	80 000		Increase by 20 000 per year	
20 000 000	150 000		Increase by 50 000 per year	Increase by 0.25%
15 000 000	100 000			Decrease by 0.1%

5   Assuming that b = birth rate, d = death rate, which of the following would apply when a population was growing? Circle the correct answer.

b > d   b < d   b = d

6   The stacked (divided) bar chart in Figure 8.7 shows life expectancy on five continents ('Americas' refers to both North and South America) in 1950, 1975, 2000 and the most recent data for 2021.

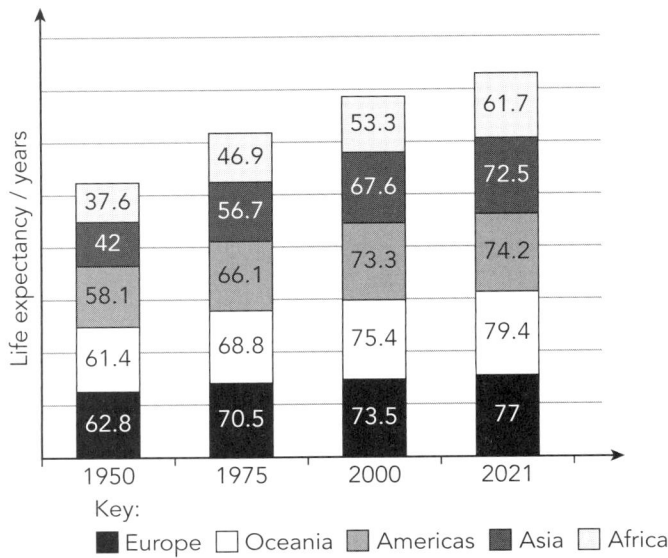

Figure 8.7: Life expectancy by continent.

Describe the trends in life expectancy on the five continents and in the world as a whole.

....

....

....

....

....

....

....

....

> Factors affecting population size

Exercise 8.4

LEARNING INTENTIONS

In this exercise you will:

- identify and explain **push** and **pull factors**
- consider factors relating to **urbanisation**
- record population data on a graph
- explore the relationship between education and birth rate.

KEY WORDS

push factors: factors that encourage people to move away from an area

pull factors: factors that encourage people to move into an area

urbanisation: an increase in the percentage of people living in urban areas

immigration: the act of moving into a country to live

emigration: the act of leaving a country permanently to go and live in another

1 a Populations change in size due to migration, which includes **immigration** and **emigration**. Write the push factors and pull factors in the correct column of the table.

- Not enough jobs
- Attractive climate
- Poor medical care
- Desertification
- Better educational opportunities
- More services and amenities
- Drought
- Better job opportunities
- Political freedom
- High levels of pollution
- Poor housing
- War

Push factors	Pull factors

b   Which type of factor, push or pull, would be most important in an LIC? Explain your answer.

....

....

....

....

....

2   The following passage describes changes in a delta town affected by dam building on the river.

In 1985, the river here was 4 km wide but is now only about 300 m. Up until about 1985 the summer floods deposited silt every year. Now, the sea is entering the delta land and many soils are useless for farming. Apart from farming, the region used to get its main income from fishing and shrimp collecting. The only fishermen remaining now catch a few crabs at sea. Most people spend the day collecting firewood.

Environmental Management 0680/22, Paper 2 October/November

This delta town has seen its population fall from 14000 in 1980 to fewer than 2500 now. Explain whether push or pull factors are likely to account for this migration from the town.

....

....

....

....

....

....

3 Identify three impacts of human population growth relating to urban areas.

a ....

b ....

c ....

> **TIP**
>
> If you are not sure how much to write in your response to a question, take the number of marks as a guide.

4 A country with a population of 11 million had 82% living in urban areas. Calculate the number of people living in rural areas in this country.

....

....

5 Birth rates vary depending on a number of factors, including the number of years females spend in education. The results of a study into how female education relates to birth rates are shown in Figure 8.8.

> **TIP**
>
> When answering questions that ask the extent to which you agree with a statement, try to offer a balanced argument. This means giving at least one argument on one side and one on the other.

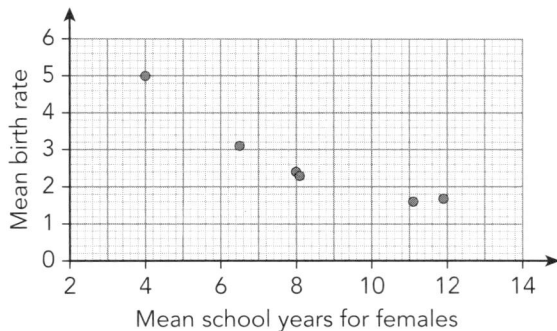

Figure 8.8: Results of a study on education and birth rates.

a Draw a line though the points where you think it would best be put.

b 'These results support the view that if girls get more education, birth rates will fall.' To what extent do you agree with this statement?

c What are the benefits and limitations of education for women in relation to human population growth?

> Managing human populations
Exercise 8.5

LEARNING INTENTIONS

In this exercise you will:

- explain how education can limit population growth

- demonstrate your understanding of key terminology

- explain factors that link birth rates and death rates

- record and analyse data from a questionnaire survey.

KEY WORD

pronatalist policy: a national or regional policy that aims to encourage couples to have children

1   Give **three** ways in which education may limit population growth.

a   ....

....

b   ....

....

c   ....

....

2   Explain the difference between family planning and contraception.

....

....

....

....

....

....

3   Explain why measures that reduce death rates, such as improving sanitation,
may also lead to a decrease in birth rate.

....

....

....

....

....

....

4   Give **two** reasons, apart from contraception, why population growth rates are low
in MICs.

a   ....

....

b   ....

....

5   Suggest why a country may adopt a **pro-natalist policy** to manage its population.

....

....

....

....

....

....

6 A questionnaire asked people in a European country if they supported stricter border controls to help manage migration. The results are shown in the pie chart in Figure 8.9 as percentages of all those asked (the respondents).

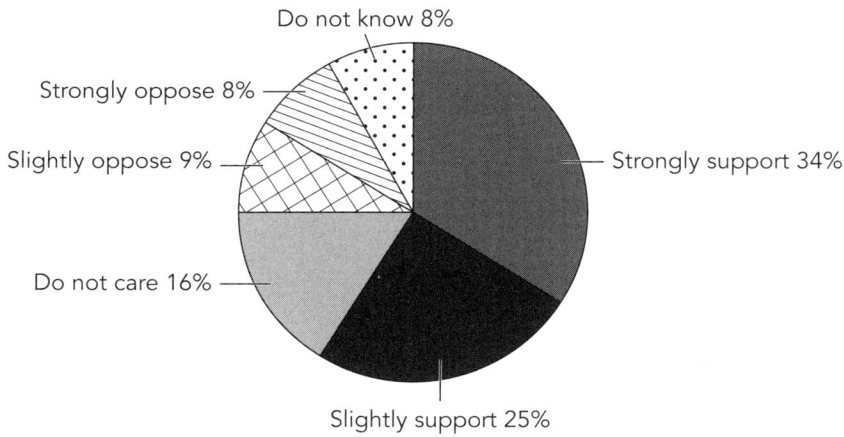

Figure 8.9: Pie chart showing the results of a questionnaire survey about border controls.

a Draw a bar chart on the grid to show these data.

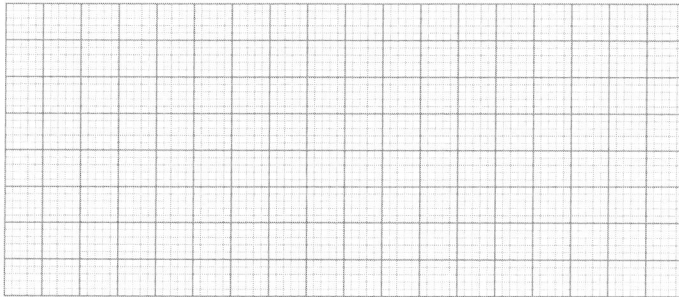

b What further information would you need about the respondents to analyse the data fully?

....

....

....

....

....

> Glossary

abiotic: non-living components of the environment that may affect living things

acid rain: rain that has been made more acidic by the presence of sulfur dioxide and oxides of nitrogen

agriculture: the cultivation of animals, plants and fungi for food and other products used to sustain human life

aim: the purpose of an investigation

algae: plant-like, photosynthetic organisms that lack true stems, roots and leaves

algal bloom: the rapid growth of algae in water, caused particularly by a surge of nutrients

aquifer: water that is stored in porous rocks under the ground

bar chart: a graph showing the relationship between a categoric variable and a quantitative variable

biotic: living components of the environment that may affect other living things

blue hydrogen: hydrogen produced from natural gas

bycatch: animals caught by fishers that are not the intended target of the fishing effort

climate: the weather conditions in a location based on the weather over many years

condensation: the process in which water vapour turns into liquid water – the opposite of evaporation

conservation: the protection and management of natural areas

continental shelf: a shelf at the bottom of the ocean near the coast of a continent, where the sea is not very deep

control variable: in an experiment, a factor that is kept constant

correlation: a pattern between two variables

dependent variable: the variable that is measured in an experiment

directly proportional: occurs when one value increases and the other value also increases

ecosystem: all the living things (biotic components) together with all the non-living things (abiotic components) in an area

ecotourism: tourism in which the participants travel to see the natural world, ideally in a sustainable way

emigration: the process of leaving a country permanently to go and live in another

enhanced greenhouse effect: when human activities increase the warming effect of the natural greenhouse effect

erosion: the movement of rock and soil fragments to different locations

food web: a diagram showing the relationship between all (or most) of the producers, primary, secondary and tertiary consumers in an ecosystem

fossil fuel: a carbon-based fuel, formed over many millions of years from the decay of living matter

fracking: the common term for hydraulic fracking – the process of obtaining petroleum or natural gas from shale rock by the breaking open of rocks using water, sand and chemicals

green hydrogen: hydrogen produced from the splitting of water molecules

greenhouse gas: a gas that absorbs radiation and emits the energy as thermal or heat energy, such as carbon dioxide, methane, nitrous oxides and water vapour

herbivore: another name for primary consumer

humus: dark earth made of organic matter such as decayed leaves and plants

hydro-electric: the generation of electricity using flowing water

hypothesis: a statement on a topic being investigated

igneous rock: rock made during volcanic processes

immigration: the act of moving into a country to live

impermeable: describing rock that water (or other liquids or gases) cannot pass through

income: money received over a stated time period

independent variable: the variable that is deliberately changed in an experiment

infiltration: the process by which water seeps into the ground

interception: the process by which precipitation is stopped from reaching the ground surface by the presence of trees and other plants

inversely proportional: occurs when one value increases and the other decreases

irrigation: the addition or water to a soil

leaching: the movement of a soluble chemical or mineral away from soil, usually caused by the action of rainwater

line graph: a graph showing the relationship between two quantitative variables

malnutrition: not having enough of the correct nutrients to eat, causing ill health

mantle: the mantle is found between the crust and core and is the thickest section of the Earth.

mean: the total of all values divided by the total number of values

monoculture: the practice of growing only one crop or keeping only one type of animal on an area of farmland

natural gas: a naturally occurring flammable gas that contains carbon; the most common example of natural gas is methane

non-renewable (finite): a natural resource that is being used up faster than it is being replaced so it will eventually run out

nutrient enrichment: an increase in the level of nutrients in a habitat or ecosystem

pest: an animal that attacks or feeds on a plant

pesticide: a chemical used control pests but also, less accurately, used as a collective term to describe pest- and disease-killing chemicals

petroleum: a liquid mixture of carbon-containing chemicals that is present in some rocks, which is extracted and refined to produce fuels such as petrol and diesel oil

pH scale: a measure of the acidity or alkalinity of a substance such as the soil

photosynthesis: the process by which plants or plant-like organisms make food in the form of carbohydrate from carbon dioxide and water using energy from sunlight

population pyramid: a diagram that shows the proportion of the population that is male and female in different age groups (usually five-year intervals)

population: all the organisms of one species living in a defined area

potable: safe to drink

precipitation: the process in which liquid water (as rain) or ice particles (as snow or hail) fall to Earth due to gravity

pronatalist policy: a national or regional policy that aims to encourage couples to have children

pull factors: factors that encourage people to move into an area

push factors: factors that encourage people to move away from an area

pyramid of energy: a diagram that represents the energy found at different trophic levels of an ecosystem

pyramid of numbers: a diagram that represents the numbers of organisms at each feeding (trophic) level in an ecosystem by a horizontal bar whose length is proportional to the numbers at that level

pyroclastic flows: very hot gases, ash and fragmented rocks, which can reach speeds of over 100 km h^{-1} at temperatures of 200°C to 700°C

questionnaire: a written list of questions that people are asked so that information can be collected

random sampling: a sampling method in which the sampling device is placed using random number tables or a random number generator

range: the difference between the largest and smallest values in a set of data

renewable: an item or resource that will not be used up or can be replaced; also referred to as a non-finite resource

reservoir: an artificial lake where water can be stored

respiration: the process by which living things release energy from food to carry out the processes of life, such as movement

rock cycle: a representation of the changes between the three rock types and the processes causing them

sampling strategy: the way in which data is collected, either randomly or systematically

sampling technique: the method of collecting data in an investigation

scatter graph: a graph with points representing amounts or numbers on it, often with a line joining the points

sedimentary rock: a rock formed from material derived from the weathering of other rocks or the accumulation of dead plants and animals

solar power: harnessing energy from sunlight

systematic sampling: a sampling method in which the sampling device is placed along a line or some other pre-determined pattern, the most common pattern being the line of a transect

transect: a sampling method in which sampling devices are laid out along a line already placed across an area

transpiration: the movement of water up plants and its subsequent loss as water vapour from their leaves

transportation: the process by which rock particles are moved to another location

trend: a general pattern in data showing an increase, decrease or remaining constant, when smaller changes are ignored

tsunami: a large, fast-moving wave created by ocean floor displacement or landslides

turbine: a machine, often containing fins, that is made to revolve by the use of gas, steam or air

ultraviolet radiation: harmful rays from the Sun

urbanisation: an increase in the percentage of people living in urban areas

vector: an organism that carries a disease-producing organism

wave power: the use of changes in the height of a body of water to generate electricity

weather: the day-to-day conditions of the atmosphere in a location

weathering: the processes that cause rock to be broken down into smaller particles

wind power: electricity generation using a wind turbine

> Acknowledgements

The authors and publishers acknowledge the following sources of copyright material and are grateful for the permissions granted. While every effort has been made, it has not always been possible to identify the sources of all the material used, or to trace all copyright holders. If any omissions are brought to our notice, we will be happy to include the appropriate acknowledgements on reprinting.

Thanks to the following for permission to reproduce images:

Cover Gani Pradana Ongko Prastowo/GI; *Inside* **Chapter 1** Darren Robb/Getty Images; **Chapter 2** Ken Crafter; Prasit photos/Getty Images; **Chapter 3** KAMONRAT/Shutterstock